BAR NONE

BAR
NONE

A defiant little ranch girl's refusal
to give in takes her from the
mountains of Colorado to the
bench of the Supreme Court.

A True-Life Pioneer Story

Val Orr

ISBN: 978-0-9903463-0-2

Cover design by Genesis, Inc.
Book designed by Mayfly Design and typeset in the Whitman and Meta typefaces.

Printed in the United States of America
First Printing: 2014

18 17 16 15 14   5 4 3 2 1

Bar None Press
P.O. Box 336883
Greeley, CO 80633
www.valeryorr.com

Contents

Preface

The history of race relations is an enduring scar on the American psyche: visible, slow to heal, and intrusive. Current headlines show that as a nation and as individuals we remain confused over how to enable a meritocracy that both respects our racial history and offers an equitable future. But in the courtroom, attempts to remedy America's ugly, vestigial past created a new imbalance, an overcorrection whose force overpowered the individuals it sought to aid, and denied equality to others in a perverse spoils system at odds with the ideas of our country's founding.

Bar None is the story of my personal struggle against that legal system, a journey that included three trips to the United States Supreme Court, and whose efforts resulted in precedential rulings that today form a bulwark against using the power of government to play favorites among its own citizens.

My upbringing gave me strength to persevere through that twelve-year struggle: a childhood continuing four generations of Colorado cattle ranchers, dating back to my great-grandfather's 1883 homestead in the bleak antebellum frontier. It's the legacy of his pioneer spirit, and the pioneers walking among us today that embody it, to whom I dedicate this book.

Acknowledgments

The stories herein are mine. So are any mistakes. To the best of my recollection, everything in here happened exactly the way it's written down. But should you find that an objective fact disagrees with my memory, I'll take most of the blame and give the rest to the steer that kicked me in the head during preparation for the National Western Stock Show back in the late 60s. It's possible he scrambled the timeline a little. I know he left me a scar so I would remember him accurately.

In preparing *Bar None*, I spent hundreds of hours interviewing family, ranch hands, legal guides, political allies, and many other dear friends—some of whom I had not seen in decades. Reuniting with them has been as meaningful for me as capturing the stories they helped me recall.

I'm grateful for their honest and poignant memories, and for having the chance to laugh and cry together again. Without the following people, the heart of this book would not beat; their additions made my history live: Jeff Buerger, Linda Chavez, Ward Connerly, Jeff Crane, Nona Crane, Ray Hart, Jean Hinman, Ed Jones, Tom Krannawitter, Rachel Legg, Bill Linke, Gary McMahan, Mike McNulty, Pat McNulty, Tim McWilliams, Joe Nance, Pat O'Rourke, Clair Orr, Fred Orr, Perry Pendley, Nicole Retland, Diane Schachterle, Ray Shoop, David Schultheis, Gary Simpson, Susan "Squid" Rector, Mona Wahlert, and Todd Welch.

In addition, I extend my deepest thanks to the following individuals.

For their horse wisdom and horse sense, I owe my parents, Jack and Alta Orr, a debt I can never repay.

Ed and Susie Orr encouraged me to shoot for my dreams. Their belief and support is immeasurable. My heart bursts with love and gratitude.

My son, Ted, is my rock-solid sounding board and best hugger. His persistent and persuasive reasons to write this book reinforced my resolve to do so.

My daughter, Kendra, encouraged me with strength and insights to write an honest story. Her sense of humor in the face of adversity is a continuous inspiration.

My granddaughter, Bella, has the patience and wisdom of a saint. Over hundreds of hours, she watched me labor over every aspect of this book. For her joyful and wondrous contributions to my life, I will forever be grateful.

This book would not exist but for the expertise of Glenn Miller. A man I met in a coffee shop became my shepherd and my friend. Thanks to him my story was brought to life.

Jim Adler, a creative genius, captured the heart and soul of this book with his simple and brilliant cover design. His uniqueness has captured my heart; his big heart has captured my soul.

Carol LaBelle-Propst, photographer extraordinaire, shot hundreds of photos. Whether I was under a crystal chandelier, wielding a smoky branding iron, or on a windy mountaintop, she made it all so enjoyable.

Laurie Brock's guidance opened my mind to the world of possibilities.

Judy Nogg read the manuscript with care; it is much improved with her suggestions.

––––––

This book is richer through the humble strength of this outstanding team. I extend to all of them my unending love and gratitude.

United States Supreme Court: Oral Arguments—Adarand v Peña (Sketch by CNN sketch artist Peggy Gage)

My mother, Alta Linke, with her pet fawn at the ranch homestead

Pioneer Spirit

"Mr. Chief Justice and may it please the Court: Adarand is a small, family-owned corporation that does business in Colorado Springs, Colorado."

—SUPREME COURT TRANSCRIPTS, JANUARY 17, 1995

The chambers are smaller than I expected, and the nine justices much closer.

Justice O'Connor: "I'm talking about the findings of Congress."

Mr. Pendley: "Yes. Well, I'm trying to answer that, Justice . . . excuse me."

Justice Rehnquist won't stay seated, pacing behind his eight black-robed counterparts. They in turn are rapid-firing legalese challenges at our advocate, William Perry Pendley, Esquire, for the Plaintiff. Our hometown stalwart and pro bono champion from Denver stands alone at the lectern: one David, nine Goliaths.

It's a legal blur, high-stakes linguistic poker with much more than my business at stake.

Perry has never been on this stage before.

Mr. Pendley: "Your Honor, we—"

Justice Stevens: "That's an irrelevant factor."

The Angry White Male next to me, my husband of thirteen years, squirms in his seat and wants it to end.

But we're just getting started.

———

In 1787, at the conclusion of the Constitutional Convention in Philadelphia, where America's founders had convened in secret for months to craft our nation's cornerstone document, the crowd asked Benjamin Franklin, as he exited Independence Hall, what sort of government the delegates had created. His succinct summary: "A republic, if you can keep it."

Freedom is fragile. The Constitution is not self-correcting or self-policing. It calls for a nation of enforcers, millions of individual citizens committed to the ethics enshrined within the document, and to the principles of equality they represent, regardless of the century.

Nearly one hundred years after Franklin's caution, in the midst of the war that tore the country asunder over those principles, President Abraham Lincoln signed the 1862 Homestead Act, a law designed to encourage trailblazers to drive west of the Mississippi and carve out the American dream, 160 acres at a time.

Its premise: "A home, if you can keep it."

After filing an application for his quarter-section, a citizen who "proved it up" by living on the land, growing crops, and building a dwelling could file for a deed and claim title. But conditions on many of the western lands were harsh: bitterly cold, arid, and isolated, and only a special type of citizen would have the fortitude and ambition to tame the edges of the expansive frontier.

Only a pioneer.

In 1866, the year after the United States safeguarded slavery's abolition with the full weight of our Constitution by ratifying the Thirteenth Amendment, the year after the Amendment's sponsor had used his resolve and rhetoric to promote it, and the year after that sponsor, our country's greatest president, Abraham Lincoln, was assassinated, my great-grandfather arrived in New York.

In that city, the *New York Tribune* editor Horace Greeley had recently published his famous editorial, imploring, "Go west, young man, go west." Soon enough my ancestor Emil Linke followed that advice, but not because he read it, or even because he heard it. When he arrived he spoke no English.

He set foot in this country a nineteen-year-old, jobless immigrant, exiled by his home country for refusing to join their dictatorial military. His language was German. His mother was black. His talent was carpentry. And his pioneer spirit took him west.

In Colorado he found a home for his interests: an interest in a silver mine, in a brothel, in German high society, and in the grape. He also found a wife, Fraulein Sophie Weil, my great-grandmother. She redirected his interests.

In 1883, relying on Lincoln's Homestead Act, Emil and Sophie Linke filed their patent for Colorado's Section 24, Township 1 North, Range 77, the original Linke ranch.

Even the Ute Indians were not as hardy and industrious as my great-grandparents. Native Americans found winters on that property too harsh, and only visited in the warmer months. But they would not be returning to their summer camps on the ranch's high peaks, not ever again. They had been driven to Utah the year prior, following congressional retaliation for recent violence over continued encroachment on Indian land. The Utes were gone, but for hundreds of years they had hunted buffalo and summered there, leaving countless arrowheads, buffalo horns, and teepee rings as evidence—artifacts of endless fascination and delight to ranch tomboys for decades to come.

Emil and Sophie endured hardscrabble years to prove up their claim, felling logs for cabins, barns, corrals, and rail-fences; hand-grubbing sagebrush to clear meadows; surveying and trenching ditches to

Linke homestead, early 1900s

allocate precious high-country water; and disproving neighbors who expected the couple to be frozen out, dried out, or starved out.

The Linkes endured, and created a family, and prospered. As the family grew, carpenter Emil built. Onto his original long log-house he added a cabin for each child. When enough children were school-aged, he built a separate log cabin, a schoolhouse for which he hired a teacher to augment his ranch staff, and whose pine walls would outlive him and all of his children, even if those log walls were not always treated with dignity.

Over time the Linke children claimed and proved up their own homesteads, and the family acquired land from neighbors of less durable constitution. Hundreds of acres. Thousands of acres.

Enough land for his son, Edwin, to raise sheep and cattle after returning from World War I, continuing his father's example of clearing sage, routing water, and tending stock with little more than a shovel and pitchfork. Enough land for my Grandpa Ed and his wife Susie to raise their own two children, my Uncle Eddie and my mother, Alta Ruth Linke.

My forebears created wealth from nothing but courage, a sense of adventure, and hard, hard work. They prospered through an unflinching self-confidence put into action, and earned respect by persevering with a self-sufficient vision to create something better. They survived by relying on a deep trust in themselves, and created a legacy of uncompromising pioneer values.

A family legacy that lasts to this day.

———

I grew up on the ranch cultivated by those efforts, an early youth on horseback and foot, and whether from intent or benign neglect, I was left unsupervised to roam it and find adventure.

I didn't feel ignored when set free after breakfast; I felt liberated. But I never left without provisions. By midday, with the sun and hunger at peak, I would always find that my mother had filled the saddlebags with salt water taffy. Of course I didn't need to carry water; it was already in every ditch and muddy creek, the occasional leech a trivial impediment.

Days spent trapped in a formal classroom dragged on. Days lived free in the saddle raced by, usually at a gallop, flushing sudden flights of birds aloft from the tall-grass meadows, racing to Ute-haunted hilltops, and jumping Nine Mile Creek, all to land at my favorite stand of Rocky Mountain willows.

At that copse, next to the creek bed, near a repurposed one-room schoolhouse, I loosed my horse to graze. Here in my high mountain castle of tree forts and willow-switches, I lay in the tall Timothy grass, imagined futures and kingdoms in the clouds, embraced a burgeoning and inexorable sense of purpose, and dreamed big dreams.

———

"Valery Jean, let's get the heck out of here." My mother's invitation to escape the July Fourth rodeo in Steamboat Springs needed no repeating, especially since she pronounced my middle name "Zhean," the French way, after my namesake in *Les Misérables*. That softer sound always meant good news. In moments we were off the bleachers, where for hours we had watched my brothers, my father, and too many other cowpokes ridin', ropin', headin', and heelin' at the biggest of the western slope rodeos. We had come to the summer event every year that I could remember, each time as much fuss as Christmas— especially for the talented Orr clan—but with too much dust and not enough snow. One always dolled up for the event: my mother and I sported matching summer dresses, bold cherries on white for this special occasion. Generally I wore britches. Dresses were not everyday wear, serving either as punishment within the confines of a school desk or grist for the dream of a lady's life.

We found shade under a broad oak near the Yampa River, the green grass there a cool invitation for us to set shoes aside and nestle into it, despite its threat of stain. She pulled out a book, one whose coral cover I recognized as part of our family library, part of the Great Books for Children collection I had been eyeing.

Alta Orr opened *Heidi*, and began with the preface. "Character grows from ideals. It is caught by contagion."

I was transported. I watched the clouds roll overhead and felt the story, dreaming as the words flowed. I loved hearing my mother read about a happy little girl who lived on the mountain. A girl like me.

At home we had our own mountain, our Rocky Mountain analog to Heidi's Alps. To me, one part of the ridge west of our ranch looked like a saddle. I pictured the highest part as the saddle horn, and could even make out stirrups, if I let my imagination work the mountains the way it did the clouds.

My mother often said she sometimes rode all the way up there, just to feel the nature all around, and nobody else at all.

———

I know that pioneers walk among us today. I've seen them: speaking their principles on the Floor of the United States House of Representatives, singing colorblind hymns solely for the music's intrinsic joy and truth, welding joints strong enough to tame a wilderness, leading a classroom with independence and passion, and shrugging off the indecencies of a racism so vile it tears families in two.

Pioneers embody relentless focus and fierce independence. They believe in themselves and persevere, relying on ingenuity and hardiness. Pioneers blaze trails with abandon and damn the cost. Pioneers make things and go places, and not usually for a larger cause.

But sometimes it just turns out that way. Sometimes, a cause finds them.

———

In 1961 my father and his family disputed how to divide the DeBerard family estate, his maternal grandfather's: thousands of acres of active Colorado ranch land, its buildings, and its championship Hereford bloodlines. Plus some metal, a set of three-foot-long, rough-hewn iron rods, their business end a matched circle and bar, scarred from hundreds of hours in the fire and on the hide.

My father chose the brand.

The Bar None brand means more than livestock or acreage. It's an indelible claim on the American Dream. It's also a promise, one that as I grew older I intended to keep, even if, as I discovered, I had to clear the road myself.

At age six, making faces

"Hasn't Learned to Sit Back Down"

"Val is standing in crib. Hasn't learned to sit back down."

ALTA ORR'S JOURNAL: MARCH 27, 1956

November 22, 1963.

I saw the glint from a block away, the high-noon sparkle off the turquoise fins of our '59 Chevy wagon. It wasn't usually parked in front of the house. The four-block walk from school each day for lunch had long ceased being an adventure, once I'd mapped every gulley, cattle track, snowbank, and stray hound that a high-plains winter signaled. But our car was in front, not yet tucked away for its Christmas hibernation. The day was unusually warm. I didn't need a coat over the navy skirt and sweater my Grandma Susie had hand-made for me. Birthday presents.

Tinny AM squalls reached the end of our rutted dirt driveway, the somber tenor of a newscast apparent as I approached. My mother should have been inside the house, waiting with lunch on the table: peanut butter and jelly, chicken noodle soup. Instead I saw her silhouette, back ramrod straight, chin up, hands at ten and two, hair coiled high in her "bird's nest" braid.

She did not move.

The driver's-side door was ajar, its window hand-cranked down. Intermittent murmuring jostled the speakers awake. I crossed my eight-year-old arms over the top of the door and saw that her knuckles were white and her eyes were red. And wet. "What are you doing?"

She blinked too deliberately. "Jack Kennedy. The President."

I waited. Such an important man. I liked him and his family.

"He's. Been. Shot."

That was Friday.

That afternoon, back at school, I huddled and murmured with my third-grade classmates as we whispered our scant details and shared our common worries. I thought it odd that our teacher made no announcement or explanation, leaving thirty confused eight-year-olds to their own private fears. I tried to imagine what the Kennedy children must be feeling, and wondered if I were alone in thinking about them more than what the shooting meant for our country. I ran home when the bell finally sounded to find my mom glued to the television, where I nestled next to her, wrapped my arms around my knees, and watched.

Over the weekend and through Monday, I perched on the center of our curved, bamboo sofa, vision narrowed to the solemn black-and-white of our Motorola's eleven-inch screen, a sad, small girl, huddling inside my horseshoe-patterned flannel blanket. Sad for Mrs. Kennedy, her black veil wind-tossed as she walked behind the casket. Sad for Caroline, who was just younger than me, and for John John, whose third birthday celebration was postponed two weeks until the Kennedy's last day in the White House. Sad for America as the bands and cortege rolled on. Sad for hours.

After the funeral, on the steps of St. Matthew's Cathedral, John John saluted his father's flag-draped casket. I tried to imagine what he and his sister were feeling, the anguish at seeing your father murdered on television, the rawness of burying him in public. The least I could do was salute with him.

When I moved to Arlington in 2002, I purchased at The Belvedere

Condominiums, across the street from Arlington Cemetery where President Kennedy was buried that day, the day Jackie Kennedy lit his eternal flame. When I lived at The Belvedere, my favorite walk was to a lookout just up the hill from the site, overlooking his grave and exposing a vista of Memorial Bridge and Washington D.C. Each time I was there I remembered seeing the bridge over the Potomac for the first time on TV, as the President's limber and caisson crossed, followed by riderless "Black Jack," boots backwards in his stirrups, all leading to his name and a simple cross on gray slate. I remembered how angry I became that someone could do this. I remembered thinking how simple the grave was for such an important man. I remembered that when I left for school that Friday morning, he was alive.

I considered how fragile freedom can be, how quickly it can be jeopardized, and how an instant can change a country and a little girl.

———

One day soon after Kennedy's assassination, I was staying at my Grandma Susie's little log house, a tidy and compact structure on our Granby ranch. I had my own bedroom there, given how often I shared her company and culture.

"Valery, do you know where God lives?" she asked, continuing our discussion regarding a person's place in the world. Breakfast was over; we had put away dishes together, and now I watched her make my bed.

"Right here, inside of me," I said without hesitation, tapping my hand over my heart. "That's where God lives." I believed, even then, that God made me the individual I was, and that I could be anything He intended me to be. I knew that I was not alone, and that I would never be alone: I have me—unique, individual me—and I have God. Our whole nation does. Our whole nation of individuals, imbued with morality and an innate sense of fairness.

Grandma might have been expecting a more celestial answer, but she accepted mine with a tilt of her head and a smile. "Yes, Dear." She fluffed the feather pillow. "You've figured out what most adults haven't, that God does live inside each of us. Yes, I suppose he does."

Grainy, haunting images put that belief to the test.

Violent upheaval, primarily in Birmingham, Alabama, but also throughout the country, signaled the deep racial chasm that still separated blacks from whites in America, and that gulf was thrust into our living rooms, to play out in fuzzy miniature on the nation's collective electronic eye.

We saw dogs snarling at protestors, police using tear gas and cattle prods to break up crowds, fire hoses turned on civil rights marchers, and bloody attacks by whites against African Americans. Although frightened by the images, I admired the courage of those taking a stand and connected with their fight to be treated fairly.

How could this be happening in America? I knew from the Declaration of Independence that all men are created equal. I knew it. And yet we were clearly treating blacks unfairly, in deeply institutionalized and ugly ways. In Grand County everyone was white, yet it was always apparent to me that treating someone different because of darker skin was wrong. Why couldn't everyone see this?

But everyone could not and would not—not without the force of law. The country, despite its harsh divisions, demanded change. So after a protracted legislative struggle, on July 2, Lyndon Johnson followed through with John F. Kennedy's signature legislation and signed the Civil Rights Act of 1964. Meant to outlaw major forms of discrimination in employment and public accommodations, as well as to address voting barriers and other inequities, the Civil Rights Act also authorized the creation of the Equal Employment Opportunity Commission (EEOC) for the Act's enforcement.

Authority for the Civil Rights Act came mostly from the "equal protection" clause of the 14th Amendment (an overreaching interpretation of the Constitution's commerce clause also supported some of the Act's more controversial features—those intruding into private businesses).

But over time, the promise of equal protection became an instrument of unequal preference. Words that should have supported fairness were turned on their head. The Act's intent was to use the power of government to create a more race-neutral, gender-neutral society—to fight discrimination. What I would discover twenty-five years later, and spend the following twelve years fighting in court, was that instead it created just the opposite: a thicket of government-sponsored discrimination so pervasive and entrenched that it still survives today.

But a nine-year-old girl had no interest in legislative minutiae; she just wanted to dream her dreams and find her heroes.

Other children believed in Santa, and worked to stay on his "nice" list. I believed in Barry Goldwater. In his speech at the 1964 Republican National Convention, he spoke of self-reliance and patriotism in ways so clear that I knew they had to be true. I sat intent, hearing Goldwater and Ronald Reagan advance principles that struck me as a call to arms, values I would later come to recognize as echoing the founding principles of our nation.

One of Goldwater's commercials asked viewers to "join me in proving that every man, every American, can stand on his own, make up his own mind, chart his own future." Determined to demonstrate my convictions, in my head I added, "and make her own bed"—something I had rarely done prior. Self-reliant people take care of their own things.

I announced my new resolution to my parents the morning after the convention. "I believe in what Barry Goldwater said," I told them, "and as long as I believe in him and what he stands for, I'm going to make my bed every day." At the time such a promise seemed the height of commitment to the principles of being a conservative, of living in accordance with what is in your heart. But my father had always told me that if a thing needs doing—if you ought to pick up a rusty nail in your path so a steer won't step on it—then "By God, you do it!"

So I made my bed. Every day since.

I also vandalized my neighbors' cars. At the time I was convinced

I was performing an important public service, but not everyone saw it that way.

I felt that the ideas I heard on television, Barry Goldwater's conservative ideas, had defined me. In some specific and personal way, they had set forth the truth for how we all ought to act: that we should respect each other, defend our country, trust God, rely on ourselves, and prosper together.

Independently, my mother and my Aunt Jean were canvassing the county on his behalf, knocking on doors, making calls, and working to rebut the democratic story that Goldwater was too conservative—too extreme—for even the frontier-minded, independent folk of Grand County. So when my mother and her sister-in-law established a booth at the county fair during the second week of September to distribute Goldwater pins and bumper stickers, I felt part of a larger team, a team with a mission and a stack of old-school, high-adhesive, permanent bumper stickers.

Along with a parking lot full of chrome.

Alta and Aunt Jean were in heated discussion with fair-goers when I depleted their pile of stickers. I was doing them and the rest of Kremmling a favor, I was sure, as I dashed from car to car. I couldn't imagine why everyone else in town wouldn't believe as I did. Why wouldn't they brand their car, just as my mother had, just as my father branded his cattle? I helped them out. Peel, stick. Peel, stick. Peel, stick.

The Grand County Fairgrounds includes a tiny show arena with five close-packed rows of bleachers. At capacity it held perhaps a hundred spectators. In years to come, showing Orr cattle in that arena, I would accumulate championship ribbons there, earning cheers from what seemed like thousands. Today, the arena was likewise full, leaving the fair buildings, the show barns, even the lampposts less attended. Certainly the buildings and the posts deserved to show their support no less than the cars did.

Stickers on. Peel, stick. Just doing my duty.

Car owners in the nearby town square were more vigilant. As I began exercising my civic responsibility there, barely a dozen instances of devout and universal patriotism into my mission, I heard what sounded like a reprimand from a woman perhaps my mother's age. "That is quite enough!" She looked familiar, but so did everyone else in town. She was nearing her car just as I was about to help her display her deepest philosophical beliefs via PVC and glue.

"You want to put your own on?" I asked, holding out her sticker. "Here you go."

"I most certainly do not want to—and you can't do this to other people's cars."

I had no idea.

"Valery Orr. Where is your mother?" Most people knew most people in Kremmling. "I'll have a word with her." Of course I told her where Alta was. People tell the truth.

I dawdled on our long march back to the fairgrounds, enough to hear only "Oh, I'll take care of it!" from my mother. She sounded angry. I steeled myself for a lashing as my captor harrumphed past me back to her unbranded car.

It had not occurred to me to ask permission. Now I started to worry about the consequences of overlooking that detail. Extra work? The hairbrush? At our Goldwater booth I readied for penance, studying the dust on my shoes, hating the silence.

I did not expect the laughter.

"Val, that's just wonderful!" said Aunt Jean, when she could finally catch her breath. "You are certainly your mother's daughter."

Was that pride I saw in my mother's face? It was definitely not anger.

Jean dropped into a conspiratorial tone. "When Alta and I visited her last week to talk about Goldwater, that 'lady' slammed the door in our face and called us everything but white women. Next time, see if you can get the sticker on before she spots you!"

———

On the Tuesday following the first Monday of November in 1964, Barry Goldwater did not win the office of President of the United States of America. He instead lost dramatically and unambiguously, carrying but six states and receiving only 38.5% of the popular vote, the lowest ratio before or since. I was stunned and heartsick after working so hard and believing so much.

His opponents had successfully cast him as an extremist, a sentiment he amplified when he capped his acceptance speech as the Republican nominee for president with a line from Cicero: "Extremism in the defense of liberty is no vice; . . . moderation in the pursuit of justice is no virtue." With his staunch conservative stances, Goldwater had not only energized Lyndon Johnson's supporters, but had also alienated many moderates in the Republican party, causing them to stay at home on polling day.

The most lasting image from the 1964 campaign, the iconic "Daisy" commercial, where a little girl dissolves in nuclear fire after an ominous voiceover countdown, played on those perceptions. And while as an advertisement *per se* it was broadcast only once, on NBC's *Monday Night at the Movies*, both CBS and ABC replayed and analyzed it thereafter. That's when I saw it.

It frightened people. It frightened me. I imagined being that little girl, and feared that our country was under attack, that our nation's destruction was imminent. As political theater, as part of Johnson's campaign to portray Goldwater as too conservative, the commercial was effective; as a memory imprinted on a nine-year-old rancher's daughter, it still haunts me today.

Yet another image haunts me more, one not from the small screen, but from the large. Movies at the single theater in town were treats for us in the mid-60s, even when the feature was as epic and beyond my scope as *Dr. Zhivago*, a big-screen spectacle of my mother's choosing. I was mostly lost by the Russian politics and love triangles, but its images of collectivized workers frightened me more than any celluloid monster would have. The workers, effectively owned by the state, all had the same look on their faces: light gone, will suppressed, trudging joyless through each day, without hope of freedom or happiness.

In the face of such bleakness, I was grateful to be born in a free nation, but I still felt that there had to be a balance between the mayhem of our country's current civil rights unrest and the soulless compliance of the Russian drones. There had to be a place where individuals were valued and where fairness mattered—and it had to be in America.

At the age of eight, when my president was assassinated, I learned how fragile our freedoms can be.

From Goldwater's acceptance speech, where he explained that during Democratic years "a billion persons were cast into Communist captivity," I learned the magnitude of the encroaching threat to the liberties of people across the planet.

From the silver screen I learned the human cost of collectivism— that look of bondage that even today I see on American faces, as too many citizens, by their apathy and willingness to live a cared-for life, embrace the institutionalized, insidious, and inexorable destruction of the human spirit.

But sometimes my worries were not as big as all that. Sometimes my biggest concern was just finding my parents.

Happy Hallmark, Orr sheepherder, at our moss rock fireplace

A Lot of Bars
and Very Few Banks

"We spent a lot of time, as kids, going to find you at the bar."

VALERY ORR, TO ALTA ORR

My father, Jack, grew up with cattle in the 1930's, in Colorado's desolate high country. One evening after harsh hours in the saddle, on the way back to the homestead after working a drive with his father—my Grandpa Ted—and the other ranch hands, Jack's mount twisted underneath him and slammed my father's knee into a stout lodgepole pine.

He couldn't find the stirrup with his boot, and almost came unseated. His eyes filled with tears. "Dad, it hurts," he sobbed.

"Quit your crying and start acting your age. We've got cattle to run," Ted said.

Jack was four.

And it never got easier for him.

Through his entire youth he ranched for his father and for his maternal grandfather, Fred DeBerard, himself a champion Hereford breeder for decades. Jack ran the DeBerard herd by the time he was in high school.

He didn't have a childhood—he had an apprenticeship.

When Jack graduated West Grand High School, he already had a cattle herd of commercial and purebred Herefords of his own, the trust of his family, and his eye on his future bride, who had just completed her first year of college. My dad likes to say that he proposed on one knee in the willows of our family's Granby ranch; my mom insists that he stayed standing so the marsh wouldn't soak his britches. They were both eighteen when they wed.

Nor did they have much opportunity to move past the confines of ranch life. Within their first year at Colorado State University together, my father was called back home. Fred DeBerard had fallen ill, and it fell to Jack to run my great-grandfather's ranch.

Instead of attending college, he and my mother started a family and managed a ranch. But even though it was a family business, it was still a business. So when, three years later, Jack was offered the job of running the Three Rivers Ranch, an hour north in Walden, he and Alta approached Fred.

"If you'll at least match their offer, I'll stay," he told his grandfather. It was winter; neither he nor my mother relished a move in the snow, especially with me just an infant and my brother only two years old. But the money was good. Jack had already abandoned college aspirations, and had until then limited his ranching ambition to no further than the property line, and to no cattle that weren't from family champion bloodlines.

But the money was good.

Fred DeBerard, 1951's Stockman of the Year, looked at his long-term right-hand man, the boy who at sixteen represented DeBerard cattle in Chicago so that Fred could simultaneously show in Omaha. (Jack won Grand Champion pen, Fred the Reserve.) He considered his 20,000 acres and 1600 registered Herefords, and the boy who had grown up at his side to run it all.

"Hm. Better take the job." All business.

We moved quickly to beat the next blizzard, our furniture tossed on a flatbed cattle truck that still had manure frozen on its bed. No time to thaw it out or wash it. Walden's winters were so severe that decades prior even the Ute and Arapaho tribes had taken to moving to lower elevations during its harshest months. Since then, failed oilmen and miners, and successful cattlemen, had boosted Walden's population to nearly a thousand rugged inhabitants.

Jack's perk as foreman of the Three Rivers Ranch was accommodations in the ranch's cookhouse, with its tiny living quarters and expansive kitchen—a cookhouse that had snowdrifts inside when we arrived, a bathroom with no heat, and a finicky coal cookstove.

The ten men he supervised needed three squares daily of meat and potatoes, all prepared over coal by the new de facto cook, ingé-

My second home, at eight months old: Three Rivers Ranch cookhouse

nue Alta Orr, age twenty-one. Although at mealtime she set places for all ten hands, often many remained unattended as workers used that break time to drink instead of showing up at table. That's because the men were drunks and hobos, vagrants gathered from Denver's Larimer Street skid row, and ne'er-do-wells shipped upslope from ragtag employment agencies. Most who arrived didn't know ranching, but they knew drinking.

Over time, most of them gave up ranching.

My mother's brief journal entries captured the fourteen months that followed before she and my father would return the hour south back to her family ranch, the Linke ranch in Granby.

> ALTA'S JOURNAL: FEBRUARY 3, 1956
> *Getting settled in is a slow process—These coal stoves are for the birds.*

Ranch owner Ruth Johnson insisted that everything be cooked from scratch on those sooty and temperamental coal stoves, including 20 pounds of bread dough, baked every other day.

> ALTA'S JOURNAL: FEBRUARY 27, 1956
> *I cleaned house, washed, baked, and fired up these damm stoves. This weather has been colder than Hell.*

Beef, slaughtered on site, is the fuel for a working cattle ranch. Supplements of flour, beans, lard, canned vegetables, canned fruit, and coffee came from weekly trips to the sole general store in town.

> ALTA'S JOURNAL: MARCH 6, 1956
> *I worked like a dog all day sorted calves, carried coal, washed, cooked. Clair put Jacks shoe in oven and it burnt up.*

Alta tried to keep the snow, manure, mud, and blood outside of the glorified log cabin in which she raised her first two children. Keeping clean inside also meant freeze-drying washed cloth diapers on the line outside or drying them inside on the iron cooktop.

> ALTA'S JOURNAL: MARCH 24, 1956
>
> *J, Dale, Cy, Bill, Charlie dehorned 420 calves. Bloody Mess. I fired Wendy when he wouldn't milk cow.*

Most of the ranch hands had bottles of rotgut secreted in boots, behind rafters, in tack rooms, and under bunks—to get by until Friday, payday, and to ease the Sunday-Monday hangover that followed every Friday-Saturday binge at the two bars in town. Needing to get the week's work started, Jack commonly used Mondays to hire other ranches' drunks who might possibly be less hungover than his ranch's drunks. Success was mixed.

> ALTA'S JOURNAL: MARCH 25, 1956
>
> *All the men left were drunk—Mrs. J. went in the air at the whole situation. . . . Two new men came. Look like screwballs.*

My grandmother Susie later said that I ran everywhere as a small girl, that I never walked. It started here.

> ALTA'S JOURNAL: MARCH 27, 1956
>
> *Val is standing in crib. Hasn't learned to sit back down. She is crawling everywhere.*

High-country haying season is short and crucial, calling always for additional seasonal help. That summer my parents cycled through more than ninety men, trying to find enough to keep the cattle tended and bring in the precious clover and Timothy hay from the fifteen-mile expanse of the Three River Ranch.

> ALTA'S JOURNAL: AUGUST 19, 1956
>
> *Same routine. Seems like there are breakdowns every day. Valery started walking.*

> ALTA'S JOURNAL: AUGUST 22, 1956
>
> *Jacks birthday—gave him 2 shirts—4 men quit this morning they had been drinking. Still haying in north field.*

Too many winos in too small a place for too long a summer eventually brought out the knives and tempers.

> ALTA'S JOURNAL: AUGUST 26, 1956
>
> *What a day. Practically all the crew is drunk. Jack got called out before breakfast to settle a fight. One of the men was a homo, and propositioned two of the boys. Two of the men were going to kill him. Jack ran him off, but not before one of the men had slugged him. Then the two that were going to kill the homo got into a fight because Clyde—one of the two—had pulled a knife on one of the other kids. All of the men that were sober were mad at those that were drunk because they came home and raised hell in the bunkhouse. Carl and Chad were drunk all day. Jack gave Carl his time [fired him] and they left. Right after dinner, Slim quit because Carl and Chad drank a bottle of his. The two kids quit because Clyde had pulled a knife on them. Clyde was passed out in the granary. There were only five of the crew left. We went to town after supper and hired back Slim and the two boys. We saw Carl and Chad in the Elk Horn drunk. We went to see the show The Birds and The Bees.*

Only the names changed as the season progressed.

> **ALTA'S JOURNAL: SEPTEMBER 13, 1956**
> *Vic, Red, and Kelsey raised Hell in the bunkhouse so Shorty left. I picked up Slim in town he quit—Jack took him in tonite. Jack fired Vic, Kelsey, and a new man that came last night. Hired back Kelsey, Chad and Red.*

For a twenty-two-year-old mother of two pressed into the role of flophouse manager, stresses compounded.

> **ALTA'S JOURNAL: OCTOBER 14, 1956**
> *Men drunk. I told Dale to get out. He pestered me all day. I got upset, went to Baker Place, had a cry—What the Hells the use—I hate ~~this pl~~ a couple of these people. Dammit I've got to get over it.*

We were still fifty miles north of any other family when winter settled in.

> **ALTA'S JOURNAL: OCTOBER 18, 1956**
> *Went to Granby and Kremmling. Jack saw DeBerard calves for Chicago—Made him homesick and me too. We shouldn't have left.*

January meant the cattlemen's Super Bowl, the Denver Stock Show. But over the preceding summer my parents had learned from their employees how one handles good times and bad times.

> **ALTA'S JOURNAL: JANUARY 17, 1957**
> *In Denver for the stock show. We went to rodeo. Took Clair. Jack partyed in afternoon. Rog Evan dumped my spaghetti in his hat and put it on a fellows head. fight ensued.*

> **ALTA'S JOURNAL: JANUARY 18, 1957**
> *Jack out at yards I went to dentist stayed loaded all day.*

> **ALTA'S JOURNAL: JANUARY 19, 1957**
> *Went to dentist then Partyed later.*

> **ALTA'S JOURNAL: JANUARY 21, 1957**
> *Came home. Damn damn damn I hated to come back to this rat-hole. Tired.*

Jack and Alta Orr moved us back to Granby in April, to a white house on the Linke ranch that I would live in for five years, until the middle of first grade.

They brought with us demons in amber bottles.

———

I grew up in towns with a lot of bars and very few banks. My parents used those buildings in proportion to their count.

Some Saturdays they would take us along to the saloon and tell us to play under the table. Other Saturdays we stayed with sitters until we eventually scared them all away. After that, once we had moved to Kremmling, we raised ourselves on weekends, scouring the local bars at sunset to find Jack and Alta solely for the money they handed us, along with some of our favorite words: "Go get something at Rudy's."

A five-and-dime with groceries, sundries, and rooms to let upstairs, Rudy's mattered to us more as the mecca of all things sweet. Four wild-west ragamuffins, dinner cash in hand, jaws agape at the possibilities. Candy bars, candy on shelves, bags of candy, barrels of candy. We did not resent our parents' weekend absences.

Not that we were faultless for the lack of supervision. By then our parents and the town had learned the folly of leaving us home with a sitter, as we worked our way through Kremmling's supply of female teenagers. The shared refrain among them became, "I'll never babysit those Orr brats again."

And with good reason: They didn't like getting tied up.

We considered it frontier justice. If instead of keeping a close eye on us a sitter remained out front kissing her boyfriend, or was (in our sole opinion) too mean to us, or simply did not amuse, then she needed taking down. Fair is fair.

It was a two-person operation. Clair helped me perch on top of the refrigerator, just beyond the kitchen doorway, high between the cabinets. "Quiet as snow," he said. "Alert as a barn cat."

Then he called the sitter in, rope hidden behind his back. When she was directly underneath me, I dropped onto her back and the two of us wrestled her to the floor. Clair hogtied her, lickety-split, two arms and one leg: much easier than a calf, and no branding iron to follow up with. We left her on the kitchen floor for our parents to find.

Years later, two of my three brothers attended college on rodeo scholarships.

As awkward as it was going to La Casa or The Hoof and Horn to find my parents, there were nights when it was worse that they were home. One night late, after we had put our younger brothers to bed downstairs, Clair and I heard our parents clatter their way in through the front door. Their voices were louder than usual—much louder.

"You and your goddamn drinking!" My father's angry shout carried an extra measure of admonition, one my brother and I had heard him use before only with intractable cattle, never with people. Never with our mother. "What the hell gets into you? You didn't used to be like that!"

"Maybe if you were home once in a while, I wouldn't need the gin to keep me company." Often Dad was home only long enough to issue ranch and household orders, and then disappear again. His real estate work kept him on the road most of the time. Recent cattle market downturns had forced Jack to look for supplemental income; his new broker's license offered possibilities.

Both of them made up for the slur of too much drink with volume. Clair and I tiptoed closer, huddling on a landing halfway between the floors. We didn't want our parents to know we were awake, but neither could we afford to miss anything important.

"Used to be we could have a good time on a Saturday night," Jack shouted. "Now, every time we go out you're picking *another* goddamn fight."

"Like it even matters to you!" Mom did not—did not ever—back down. "You drive off and do whatever you goddamn please. Leave me to rot in this hellhole with four kids to raise. You never even see them."

My older brother and I looked at each other, lost and frightened. There was familiar green shag carpeting under our feet, but nothing recognizable in the din overhead. These were not parents we knew, and for a moment I saw my pre-teen brother and my ten-year-old self as Hansel and Gretel, abandoned without our breadcrumb trail.

Jack's turn next: "It's embarrassing to be seen with you—falling all over yourself, shooting your big mouth off."

And then Alta: "If you ran the ranch better, you wouldn't need to be wasting your time with real estate and leaving it all to me here. All I've done for years is pick up after you. Do all the shit that needs done around here."

The people upstairs kept at it, kept at the volume and the frightening exchanges, kept at the visceral belligerence and the hateful drunk release, while downstairs their two eldest took small clinging solace in a shared fear, and worried what the morning and the weeks ahead might bring.

The morning and the weeks ahead brought nothing. No acknowledgment, no apologies, no retractions—nothing. Not the next morning. Not the next week. Not for twenty-five years.

When my father built the Happy Hallmark library extension onto our Kremmling house, he included a garage in his construction, separated directly from the library by a dividing wall. Dominating that wall, and protruding through both sides, was our new moss-rock fireplace.

The fireplace stood as testament to the family effort it took to gather so many *just so* skull-sized rocks from Grandpa Ted's ranch. My brothers and I clambered atop a slope on the south side of his ranch, wedged and heaved the stones one by one, and slid our candidates to our mother, far below, for approval. Then we mass-hoisted the selected rocks, properly oblong and dense, into whichever car or pick-up had been free for one of the dozens of rock runs, each carload containing the slabs she was sure would not only align best, but also present the right surface for the spray-bottle application of beer she used to feed the moss.

The fireplace stood as tribute to the weeks it took to build, and the years of heat and hearth and home it created within.

It stood as bulwark for a more complete resource library than the adjacent high school had.

Until it didn't.

Happy Hallmark was my grandfather Ted Orr's sheepherder—paunchy, Spanish, dark, not handsome. Every summer he tended Ted's herd, ranging solo in his horse-drawn sheep wagon wherever the sheep could forage, his summer home a customized covered wagon outfitted to keep one man housed and fed on the range for months. With only bleating wool and mutton for company, Happy read to pass the time, and he read voraciously, loading hundreds of new books into every cranny of the sheep wagon at the beginning of each season. For years. Until his collection grew too large to keep at the loft he rented at Rudy's, and needed a new home.

When the Grand County Library turned their nose up at the collection, my mother got creative: it was time for an addition to our house. My father built it; she painted it, red and black, and outfitted it with Mexican glass chandeliers we bought in Tijuana and with a massive library table big enough to host our holiday meals. She glued pocket sleeves in each volume and hand-wrote a library card for every one. She installed the best stereo system for miles, and then opened the doors to the community.

When school was in session, students treated the room as a literary annex, one with deep shelves and unexpected ambience, since the library always had music playing: classical selections, Henry Mancini, The Monkees, Al Hirt, Rod McKuen, the national cast of Up With People. Hundreds more, but always music.

The library was a source of pride and sanctuary for her.

Until it wasn't.

On most mornings Tippy, our scruffy Lassie wannabe, scuffled and begged underfoot while I made breakfast, hoping he had eroded my willpower enough that I might send a sausage or two his way, but this winter Sunday morning was quiet. Coffee was on, much earlier than usual; perhaps mom had the dog with her.

I found my mother in what was left of the library, her eyes as empty and stained as her coffee cup. Stone dust and black soot covered every surface: the glass chandelier, the record player, the broken coffee table, the bullfighting décor, the books and books and books everywhere. Everywhere except the pile of moss-rock rubble in the room's center. Beyond that, where our fireplace had been, the front of our station wagon now intruded, windshield and headlights in fragments, our hand-picked stones in mortared clusters on its marred hood.

"Tippy is still under my bed," she said. "He was right here last night, but when that wall went he was gone." Her face was cut—not dangerously, but the wounds had not been cleaned, nor had the soot been washed from her cheeks except by tears.

"What happened?"

Somber and monotone: "I was trying to hit the brake. Got the gas instead."

I knew she had been snowmobiling with friends the night before. I knew that any compunction against drinking and driving she may have had did not apply to those vehicles. I also knew that lately any such qualms did not actually apply to any vehicles.

"I broke it," she said, no fight in her voice. "Valery Jean, I broke it all."

———

Over the next few weeks, until we had the fireplace rebuilt, classmates arriving to borrow books put the obvious question to me. "My mom drove through the wall," I mumbled, cheeks red. But they weren't as shocked as I was embarrassed; her drinking was no mystery to other folks in town. They had seen her stumble down the bleachers, reeking of gin, when I cheered for the district wrestling tournament, her hostility on full display. They had seen how I recoiled at the spectacle, helpless in my purple-and-gold regalia and pasted smile.

It's a small town. There was talk. "I feel so bad for those Orr kids," I heard later, third-hand. But at the time I didn't want talk; I just wanted to get through high school.

A childhood echo that my brothers and I share is a phrase we heard often from my mother, purportedly joking, usually between her second and third highball of the night: "You kids drove me to drink."

We knew it wasn't true, but she didn't.

My brothers: (L to R) Clair riding Buddy; Ed riding Little Joe; Fred riding Partner

No Pink Saddles

"A milk cow does not like her teats being squeezed in the wrong way."

VALERY ORR

Having two residences was not unlike a custody situation: school years in the cocooned, scotch-and-gossip community of Kremmling, summers and long breaks working the ranch in nearby Granby, haying and grooming and riding—but always working when there, and never with concessions for age or gender or even state of health.

There were no pink saddles on the ranch, no pink helmets or pink cowboy hats signifying that gentle womenfolk need not shovel manure or move cattle. There was always work to do, more than a day's full, and the understanding that in our family everyone did as told and did it again the next day. There was neither time to relax nor any thought of affirmative action on the ranch, especially with Jack Orr as boss.

His hired crew included winos, wayward boys, and us four Orr kids. He expected less from the winos and wayward boys.

"Dad, I am really sick," I choked out, through the worst sore throat I could remember. Moving cattle to the least-grazed pasture constituted most of my early summer work, and shouting over the bellowing herd had sent sharp pains down my throat, like swallowing a porcupine. I bent low over the saddle horn, suddenly weak.

"We're moving cattle. Keep up." Echoes of his father.

I whispered to my horse, "I'm pretty sure I have a fever."

That night, country doctor Ernest Ceriani confirmed it: Strep. He scribbled the Penicillin prescription and handed it to my mother, using his cigarette as a pointer. "Alta, make sure she takes it all, and you tell Jack she gets one day off. I don't want her back here in a week." He turned to me. "Young lady, I'd ask you to rest longer, but your father would have my hide. You'll be fine soon. This medicine works fast."

I liked Doc Ceriani. Everybody did. Even *Life* magazine. Their 1948 photo essay of him chronicled his workaday exploits as the tireless, self-sufficient community caretaker, brilliantly simple in his direct approach. He had delivered most everyone in town under the age of twenty, and sewn or splinted nearly all the rest. I retain to this day a reminder of his craft: a faded scar of delicate stitches circumscribing my left thumb, his handiwork the only reason the severed digit thrived instead of died in the car door that slammed it.

On my rare doctor's-orders rest day I plotted with cousin and co-troublemaker Mona. Her parents, my Aunt Jean and Uncle Rod, had been talking with grizzled hand George Uncapher, and reminiscing over their honeymoon at George's cow camp fifteen years prior. It sounded romantic: working the high range, in the saddle all day, tending cattle and taking in the countryside on horseback—in short, everything I was already doing, but without my dad barking orders. George needed only two riders for this summer's weeklong camp, and wondered if perhaps Jean might care to send her daughter along this year. Jean asked Mona. Mona asked me. I asked Mom. Somehow, everyone said yes.

Mona and I discovered, at cow camp, that George Uncapher was a cook of limited repertoire. At first, canned chili was a novelty for breakfast. And for lunch. And then for dinner.

"Really, there's nothing else?" Mona asked him on morning two. "All week?"

"Look around, Sunshine." The two-room cabin slept George in the single bedroom, with our cots here in the "kitchen," along with a rough counter, water jugs, camp stove, and pine shelves, stocked deep and high with Hormel's chili con carne—and nothing else.

Crusty cowboy George was at home without running water, electricity, or variety. Two cowgirls could follow his model for a week, we decided: saddling up early, gathering cattle, and eating canned chili.

The outhouse, thirty steps away, became more necessary as the week wore on.

A shower became necessary too, but happened only from nature, not from plumbing. Rainclouds overhead swept in fast one afternoon, sending a murmur through the cattle and a chill through Mona and me. Pelting rain soon followed, with lightning: dangerous, open-range lightning.

"Y'all girls take cover out the rain," he said, over the rising wind and quickening thunderclaps. George wheeled his mount to point at the nearest tree, a weathered bristlecone.

Underneath the scant shelter, and already soaked through, I said to Mona, "The splits in this tree, these big black cracks, do they look like lightning damage to you?"

She saw my wide eyes, glanced over to find George sidling his mount under a similar canopy, looked around at the slate gray skies punctuated with abrupt white flashes, and put one her finger to her lips. "Shhhh."

After a week we were glad to get back home, even if it meant being around my brothers again.

A girl in a family of boys needed to work hard to keep up—not only with the ranch tasks of irrigating, animal grooming, and haying, but also with the more important tasks of keeping her brothers in their place. The only thing more annoying than uppity little cowboy whippersnappers was when those same munchkins were your own brothers.

Fred was easy. Five years younger than me, his sweet tooth and undeveloped guile created exploitable weaknesses, for which one opportune commercial offered inspiration. The TV pitch promised that Ivory liquid soap was so creamy that it would peak like whipped cream when beaten with a hand mixer. I colluded with ranch neighbor and bestest buddy Nona to put this slice of kitchen-science magic to the test one Sunday morning at Grandma Susie's.

We had the run of her kitchen, having just waved her off. A true southern lady, her church attire reflected the most genteel persona we ever saw on the ranch: smart dress, pearls, pillbox hat, low heels with a matching purse, and gloves. Always gloves.

"Try just soap—no water," said Nona, once my grandmother was reliably away. "I bet that's what they did on TV."

The commercial did not lie. In short order, brilliant white foam hung stiff on the beaters, and Grandma's stoneware bowl brimmed with fluffy mounds of promise.

Mimicking the TV announcer's baritone, I said, "It even whips!"

"Looks creamy, feels creamy," said Nona, completing the catchphrase.

"But doesn't *taste* creamy," I said. We burst into giggling peals of mischief.

We filled two sundae bowls, slid in spoons just so, and stepped outside, where my youngest brother and his playmate, that annoying Turner kid, were stockpiling dried cow flops for an eventual shootout. They needed soap anyway.

"Hey, Freddie!" I worried that my sing-song appeal might come on too strong, but the bratty little brother and the mama's boy sidled on over, eyes locked on our outstretched delights. They overlooked our uncommonly clean hands. "Here's some whipped cream for you."

Two scrawny barn tramps. Two right hands scooping giant spoonfuls. Two big bites and two hopeful swallows.

Two bowls clattering to the stoop. Four eyes rounded in shock.

They ran, Fred in a lost serpentine, as if he might find a heretofore unseen water trough into which he could submerge his entire head, the other beelining it to the Turner house, shrill cries of "Mommy, Mommy, Mommy!" receding with him.

Nona and I had never been so proud.

"Two on two," she said. "Fair is fair."

Older brother Clair was trickier. For him, I needed to appeal to his higher sense of adventure. Luckily for me, Happy Hallmark had built the trap, and a rusty lantern I had stumbled across during the prior weekend on the ranch provided the bait.

Our school year had just started, along with upcoming wrestling tryouts. I needed a distraction to keep from being used as Clair's unwilling practice dummy. I needed something else for him to do after school. I needed the Hardy Boys.

"Where'd you get that?" Clair asked, seeing the corroded relic I had positioned adjacent to my homework.

How does one hide a twinkle in the eye? "I found it." So far not a lie.

"In the tunnel." A lie.

"Out back." A big lie.

Hardy Boys mysteries comprised only a small fraction of our Happy Hallmark library, but nearly all of Clair's reading interest. The Hardy Boys always had a lantern.

"Don't tell anybody," I said. He shook his head, pursed his lips, and leaned in closer. "You dig down about six feet. There's a trap door and a whole set of tunnels once you open it, and they're just filled with all these old relics." I hunkered down over my papers. "But I'm busy here. I have so much school work."

Trap set.

The next day, dirt began to fly. For days to come Clair ran home from school and set to digging. He dug down and dug across; he dug deep, with ranch-hand stamina, each day spouting a dirt cascade as testament to his diligence. Digging the next day, and the next, each day deeper and with equal fervor. Watching through the window I wondered why it had not occurred to him to ask just how I had extracted my own archaeological find without leaving any trace. But every day he ran home again and dug again.

Every day digging was one without wrestling.

After a week, he slowed down. "Where's that trap door?" he finally asked, resigned. "I just can't find those old tunnels."

I was waiting. I had my dictionary at the ready for days, bookmarked to a certain page. "You know, Clair . . ." I said, trailing off. I tapped the entry. "Take a look."

The word was "gullible."

Clair was too much older and Fred was too much younger for a fair fight, but at two years younger than me, Ed was just the right age. So him, I just beat up.

In addition to being too young to overpower fairly, Fred was also too young to be on the hay crew, so he found his role models in whichever roustabout had barn or welding shop duty. Such duty, given the unruly beasts and decrepit equipment, generated prominent and varied lessons in swearing for young Fred: vicious, rapid-fire blue streaks for incompliant steers, barked expletives and flinging for uncooperative hand tools, and meticulous, slow-motion cussing for tractor engines.

Fred listened closely while practicing his roping.

He also heard Tippy's squeal, that disturbed yowl suggesting that perhaps the dog had, once again, mistaken a porcupine for . . . anything else. Tippy gathered momentum as he ran in from the willows.

Fred swung his oversized loop at the calf-roping dummy, twice his size and almost as dirty. Tippy, clearly seeing an invitation to fetch, jumped full on Fred's chest, sending the junior roper to the ground, backside first.

"Get away from me, you son of a bitch," said Fred, echoing the voices from the shop.

Mom burst out the door, her ire instant. "What did you say?"

Grandma Susie arrived behind Alta, scowl intact. She said to my mother, and not for the first time, "That boy's not well churched."

From the ground, pushing Tippy aside, Fred said, "I just called him a son of a bitch. So what?" Full of innocence.

"So *this*, young man." Mom snatched one dirty wrist and half-carried the young offender inside, a tirade of her own spilling forth, among which I distinctly heard, ". . . mouth out with soap."

I had some extra whipped cream if she needed it.

———

Tippy was my confidante and playmate, an ever-present companion and protector while growing up. He taught the value of loyalty—but not much else. For wisdom, we learned that from a barn-sour quarter horse.

Cupcakes who ride English and east-coasters call his copper-red color "chestnut," but it's "sorrel." Sparky was four years old, the same as my brother Clair, when Dad succumbed to horse-trader Levitt's pitch. "I got this great kids' horse," Levitt said. "Fourteen hands. Not too big. Wouldn't know how to buck if you spurred him twice." Jack knew cattle better than horseflesh.

My brothers and I all learned to ride on Sparky. We also learned to never turn our backs on him, after each receiving enough bites on the butt to remember to keep facing him and to keep an eye on his teeth, a wariness I came to value years later in Washington, D.C.

Sparky's cleverness was never in doubt, nor his sense of direction. More than once he got us back to the barn in a driving rain or deepening dark, a child's head lain against his neck, small eyes covered against wind or too tired to stay awake. But we paid a toll for Sparky's penchant. At the end of a long day moving cattle it might help if we pointed Sparky at the barn, but the puny intentions of a ranch waif ultimately did not matter. Sparky knew home. Our job was to make sure that both Dutch doors were already open when he saw it.

There was perhaps one foot of clearance between a heads-down Sparky at full gallop and the top Dutch door. I discovered, over my protests, that with reins pulled fully back and boot heels pushed fully forward in the stirrups, my vertical cross-section was nonetheless more than perhaps one foot. Any ensuing backflips on my behalf were unintentional. The lesson that day was to plan ahead and leave yourself a safe way home.

Sparky also taught us to stay the course, because he would strand us. Should any Orr youth dismount, voluntarily or otherwise, Sparky seemed to understand that reins and heels no longer applied. He cocked his head, blaze askew, surveying us for hidden grain or some other reason to remain, his look one of, "Well you dumb son of a buck. Don't you know it's miles to home?" Miles on foot, since Sparky was already gone. As a result, my brothers learned to pee standing sideways off the saddle, in stride. Lacking that option I learned to ration my resources, keep a tight rein, and prepare for a long ride.

Over time Sparky finally learned his own lesson. On this morning my father had asked but one task of his offspring: bring in the bull from the north pasture. Breeding registered Hereford cattle meant pairing cow and bull in a controlled setting and at the right time. The bull needed to come in.

My youngest brother, Fred, had the special privilege of riding Sparky. As my brothers approached their target, it became apparent that today's bull had no intention of complying with any number of children on horseback. It backed into the barbed wire, front legs locked. The oldest brother, Clair, chose the strategy. "Fred, take Sparky. Back him up to that bull."

Well out of sight of the barn, and with other horses nearby, the tractable Sparky acceded to Fred's simple maneuvering. The horse consented to the turnaround, his tail pointed to the bull from a safe forty-foot distance. Sparky set to munching a late-season tuft of grass.

From even further away, Clair said, "When he charges you, Ed and I will get in behind you and then we'll start pushing him."

Fred turned in his saddle at the bull, at its broad white face, curly forelocks, and black stubborn eyes. He had the beast's attention, but not its agreement. He looked at his brothers and flashed a grin of confidence. They waved him on.

My nine-year-old brother leaned back over the saddle and patted Sparky on the rump. "Here, bully, bully, bully, bully!" he said, full of hope and mastery.

The bull's head dropped.

Fred's jaw fell slack. He blanched. Kicked Sparky as he turned.

The charge seemed in slow motion, the bull off the fence in heavy, mean strides, head down, wide nose sneering. Fred's eyes grew wide as he faced front. Sparky ate grass, ignoring the tiny heels at his side, his measure of compliance complete for the day.

At full charge, the bull closed the distance just as Fred laid a hand on the horn, just as Sparky cocked an ear to the sound approaching behind him.

A fully grown Hereford bull tops out at upwards of 2400 pounds. Even saddled and carrying Fred, Sparky couldn't have been half that, which meant that with his front legs planted when the bull hit, his back half flew skyward, hip over withers, rear hooves rising even with the bull's shoulders, in a momentary equine handstand.

Fred flew higher than that but held on, the laws of inertia thwarted by one desperate hand clutching reins and horn. With early rodeo instinct he kept aloft just long enough to stay his mount when Sparky bounced his way back to earth.

After that, the king of the pasture snorted and puffed his way home, dominance proven. Sparky responded attentively to Fred's minimal lift of the reins and followed at a safe distance, eyes always on the bull. Clair and Ed were laughing too hard to argue about who took point.

Sparky behaved better for a time. Whatever his animal thinking may have pieced together, it seemed to me a human lesson worth remembering: "When the bull is coming at you full force, watch your ass."

———

We found guidance in unexpected places, in the expansive library of an itinerant sheepherder, and in the quiet ethic of Walt the Wino.

Short, old, laconic, and diligent, Walt Gallagher spent all of twelve summers and many of the remaining seasons at the ranch, cooking, fishing, fencing, and drinking, but mostly irrigating: rerouting our reservoir's bounty through daily ministrations of the hundreds of natural and hand-shoveled rivulets that criss-crossed our ranch, constantly chasing brown fields and turning them green. I had heard "He can make water run uphill" so often that I began to wonder if just perhaps it were true.

Walt knew his place in the world in a way that my father never did: at peace with being a hired hand for the rest of his days, resigned to needing to escape to the bottle for a near-death bender every few months, and prone to showing up after that in the same Larimer Street bowery where we first found him, having finally emptied every bottle of cheap hooch, vanilla flavoring, and rubbing alcohol he could scrounge.

The whisper at the time was that Walt's wife had been killed in Tennessee, and that his resulting escape to the bottle destroyed his nascent music career there. After the first jug of his homemade dandelion wine he would recount how he co-wrote Hank Williams 1950 hit, *Why Don't' You Love Me?* After the second, he would sing it. After the third, there was no turning back.

But this evening I didn't need music or even irrigating advice, or even Clair, who had become Walt's shadow when Dad was not around—which was most of the time. I needed The Goat, a topless army weapons carrier we had drafted into agricultural service, and branded to signify, by painting its name in rough white letters on the side. Stronger than an ATV, less demanding than a horse, and more nimble than a tractor, it became our go-to method of hauling tools, fence roll, feed, and people when available. Oats needed delivering, and the muddy, rusty, reliable, loud Goat was the best tool for the job.

Against my better judgment, I checked the bunkhouse for someone who might know the whereabouts of my favorite vehicle.

The only pretty things inside were three horizontal beams of orange light spanning the interior of the log-walled bunkhouse, evening sun lancing through the bullet holes on its west wall. From the smell and haze, Walt must have primed the wood stove with diesel fuel this morning, enough for a little heat and a lot of smoke. Everything about the spartan housing sent clear "I've got to stay away from here" signals. Eight unmade cots ringed the wall; four unmade single beds comprised the interior luxury suites; one unmade couch near the stove was the penthouse.

It smelled like sweat socks and extra boy.

Crisco cans and coffee cans, holes punched for hanging, dangled from cables looped across the rafters, a swaying mobile of too-seldom-emptied personal spittoons I had previously learned not to jostle. Teen hand Pat McNulty was rigging some Rube Goldberg improvement, a series of eye ring screws through which he rerouted the cables closest to his cot, replacing them with more functional string. He looked up from his contraption. "I thought I smelled saddle soap." He and his twin brother, Mike, seemed to keep their eyes off their work and on me a bit much when I dared venture close to the gentlemen's quarters. I walked on.

It was hard to picture how this structure had once been the schoolhouse my mother had learned to read in, a building that over time grew too shabby for formal learning, and then got shabbier enough to host life learning for my brothers and other teens from problematic homes.

I found Gary McMahan, de facto Orr babysitter, troubadour in training, and a terror to industrious beavers, feral cats, and any dwarf calves unfit to raise. Gary was always strapped and always anxious to have a reason to use his .45. He was also blessed with an authentic twang and a natural falsetto he could unleash in a yodeling master class.

"You got to be awful desperate to come nosing in here," he said, filling up a cheek with Beech-Nut. "Chew?"

"I'm not bumming that from *anybody* since you told me how Arkansas John keeps his moist so my brothers won't pester him for some." Arkansas John's single demonstration of peeing on his own stash had become legendary. Besides, tobacco turned me green, but I didn't need to announce the weakness. "I just need the Goat."

Gary pushed his mountain-man hair out of his eyes and chuckled. "Your older brother's got it." He paused for effect, his storytelling chops well developed even in his early twenties, having been honed with years of practice to the captive audience here on the ranch. "He's got it—on a date."

Oh, Lord, let me never marry a cowboy.

"I'll use the tractor."

———

Most of our calves were born in late winter; by May they needed branding, that tag-team cowboy whirlwind operation that binds, burns, cuts, vaccinates, medicates, vitaminizes, and dehorns, leaving the calf to stagger off in wobbly indignation, a few ounces lighter and determined to never leave mama cow's side again.

Branding is the two-day social event of the spring, one that used every ranch hand, relative, and neighbor we could round up, working over a communal fire and feasting later at the dinner and oyster fry. But despite its choreography and reliance on expert, unspoken teamwork, branding was not a glamorous job. These were dirty animals, pushed through crowded chutes into a muddy clearing, roped and dragged bawling from their dams, shitting for being scared or sick, bleeding from their horn stumps and abdomens, and lowing their collective separation in an all-day dirge.

In general, some of the best times of the year.

Under Jack Orr's supervision, the process was never without considerable commentary. "What the hell do you think you're doing?" he shouted, to new arrival Tim McWilliams, a scrawny teen whose grasp around the calf's neck left Tim open to being kicked and, more urgently, left the calf free to shift when the branding iron struck. Jack Orr did not abide a smudged brand. The circle and line of the Bar O brand, the Bar None brand, was simple and clean; he meant to keep it that way on the calf's left flank. Which also meant that no one besides Jack wielded the heat, and everyone but Jack damn well better keep those calves motionless underfoot.

"That's not the way you're supposed to do that!" Jack shouted. "Val, show that boy how to hold the goddamn calf." As my father set the iron back into the wood fire I showed young Tim how to hold the goddamn calf.

"Squat down over its withers—"

"Withers?" Thirteen-year-old Tim had no idea. He had shown up yesterday with a suitcase full of pilot magazines and talk of sleeping on the open range by a gentle campfire. His current shell shock belied the cowboy fantasy. Maybe if he washed out soon enough he could follow through on his aviator dreams.

"Its shoulders. Put your right knee on its neck, pull its left leg to your belly," I said. The calf had already been roped and dragged into place; we just needed to keep it on its back. "Lean into him if he gets feisty. He'll calm down." At the aft end I held the hindquarters secure, my left foot extended holding its bottom leg away, its left rear hoof in my tight, two-handed grip, hoping that this calf was not scouring or for any other reason inclined to spew pea-green crap on my face. "And when Ray gets here to cut, and Jack gets back to brand, just hold still."

Hold very still for one-eyed Ray; he flashes a knife without depth perception, using his removable glass eye only for show and surprise. More than one new arrival took Ray up on his offer to keep an eye on the rookie's hat when he stepped away, only to return and find that Ray had kept his word, literally.

Ray's castration took less than thirty seconds: quick slice for access, then stashing the bloody knife crosswise between his teeth, two free hands to find the prizes, tug and stretch the cords, snatch the knife back and cut, cut. He grinned at his handful of pink and flesh. "Finally got a pair with some size. Them others are just appetizers," he said, carrying his two oysters back to the nut bucket, those increasingly crimson gallons of water at the bottom of which hundred of testes would accrue by day's end, all destined for Aunt Virginia's beer batter.

Tim's eyes were as wide as the calf's.

Of course not every calf got cut. The call of "Got a heifer" meant we saved a step. Male calves that kept their nuts became unruly bulls, necessary for breeding and teaching lessons to Sparky, but nasty for most else, including eating: too little marbling on too much muscle. Untesticled steers are more tractable, smaller, prettier, and tastier. We didn't let many remain bulls.

But we branded every one. Dad pressed the glowing brand onto hair and hide, creating an eruption of flame and smoke so sudden it seemed caused less by heat on leather than by some pent-up subterranean venting from beneath the calf, as if the iron pierced the ground to uncork a hissing fumarole from Satan's own bloated, syphilitic scrotum.

The hissing smoke is a rancid stink of fouled steak, charred liver of roadkill, steaming dog, and diarrhhetic bear scat stew. It's the smell of a beef ashtray, of a grease fire at a yak barn. It's what skunk bacon would taste like if served wrapped around a hillbilly's used corncob. It's a sizzling campfire, just doused by latrine sludge. It's roast cow flop with a charnel edge, that clings for hours in one's nostrils.

It's not good.

And yet, towards lunchtime, as the dust rose and the smoke settled, the pervasive, hovering stench of charcoal and sewage became disturbingly appealing.

Ranch appetites are scary.

———

"God damn the god damn the sunofabitch to hell!" I didn't need to hear every syllable to recognize the refrain of Jack Orr during haying season. His response to some hand's boneheaded decision or some Orr kid's failure to mimic Dad's technique was to throw his white Stetson to the ground, jump directly on it, and undertake a red-faced stomp-and-holler tirade equal to any child's tantrum. "God damn the god damn what the hell are you doing?" What he lacked in variety of diction, he made up for in volume and duration.

The fact that we heard it often made its effects no less personal, a sentiment apparent on Clair's face as he limped the 24-foot rake back to the barn, one of its wheels canted outward, clearly destined for Grandpa Ted's welder. My older brother backhanded the dust and tears off his face as he slid down from the tractor. "I can't ever do anything right for Dad," he said. "Stay far from the ditch and he yells that I'm leaving hay standing. Drive too close and the wheel goes in."

I knew the feeling. Get seven days' work done in one, with ramshackle equipment and absentee supervision, and with no mistakes. Failure means the Rocky Mountain Call, or worse—an over-the-knee tanning whose only mitigation might be Grandpa Ed's work glove sneaked in for backside padding. Success means do it again tomorrow. No circumstance leads to approval. Not ever. Not from Jack Orr.

The closest he got to encouragement was by comparison. "Why can't you be more like Mitch and Gina?" my father said, contrasting my cousins. "Those girls are a hell of a hand on the ranch." In spirit and performance I was never a hell of a hand on the ranch.

One might imagine that someone so irritated at failure ought to ensure that his crew came with a life of ranch experience, a deep knowledge that would obviate the need for frequent corrections and hat stomping.

And yet. Lessons from his early management of the Jones ranch notwithstanding, my father was a man to give the world a second chance. He continued to hire winos from Denver's seediest skid row, and to offer ranch work as a refuge for city boys needing some country—and then he never fired them, regardless of their talent or drive. Workers often quit or failed to return for a subsequent season, but Jack Orr would not make that choice for them. Jack never let a bad hand go. Not every teen or drunk arrived prematurely hardened, but those who did found a set of rules and a work ethic that had previously been missing, and for some it made all the difference. By providing freedom with consequences, more work than a person could handle, and an unyielding commitment to staying the course, Jack rescued many lost boys and men.

But it cost him his fatherhood. Overused and undermaintained like ranch equipment, my brothers and I grew up not because of him, but in spite of him.

My first steer, Abe (for Abe Lincoln), Middle Park Fair

Black Sheep

"You will not have a nigger friend. You will not!"

GRANDPA TED

A man is standing on the moon.

"*Unglaublich.* Has to be camera tricks," my Grandpa Edwin Linke said. My mother's father, a World War I veteran, looked straight at the images of ridged bootprints and a hoisted American flag flickering on the television. "Can't be done." Grandpa Ed had never flown in a plane. His regular morning walk up our lookout hill was as close as he would ever come to the moon.

But his eyes stayed fixed on the screen. "They want you to forget about Bobby Kennedy and Martin King being shot. Vietnam. Demonstrations. This moon mission is what the government wants us to believe, so we don't think so much about the problems everywhere." He shook his head. But he didn't look away.

My grandfather's lifetime spanned the invention of the automobile to Neil Armstrong's "giant leap." This man, born to a ranch life and grown to solve every puzzle with muscle and generosity, could not accept that the world around him had changed so fundamentally that it might not fit him any more. His answer was to deny what he saw.

I couldn't do that.

What I saw was that I didn't fit in.

The role I was born into, as just another ranch hand, began to lose its inertia. As I started high school my father had just been elected the youngest president of the Colorado Cattlemen's association. More then ever, cattle became his life. His days were cattle. His nights were cattle. His children were cattle.

For years I had been showing Orr Herefords at regional shows and across the western United States. We took our family vacations in a two-ton truck with stock racks, pulling six steers and a dozen feeder calves. Other families ended up in Yellowstone or Disneyland. We vacationed at the Arizona National Livestock Show or the Ogden Livestock Exposition or the National Western Stock Show in Denver.

And we won, often enough. Good stock, good care, and good showmanship brought in ribbons, plaques, and prize sales. Other teenagers got allowances. My brothers and I got to keep the proceeds of the one steer we would each raise and show—and a champion steer could fetch thousands at the livestock sale that concluded each event. But each show reflected months of preparation, work that increasingly fell to me as my brothers grew into ranch supervisors and rodeo competitors.

My summers became an endless blur of steer care: the basics of haltering, tieing, brushing, and feeding. Hard scrubbing to get the mud and manure off. Wetting steers down to promote hair growth, then blow-drying to keep the hair pointed in the same direction. Clipping the coat to disguise any weak points. Treating any diarrhea or festering pinkeye. Training with the hooked show-stick to teach the steer to set up and stand still, planting all four hooves squarely underneath. And popping grubs.

During showing, a judge rubs his hands along the steer's back to feel its conformation and the distribution of fat and meat. A show steer needs a smooth back, not one sporting the huge, infested pimples that grubs make. A cattle grub, or warble, is the larva of the large, hairy heel fly, whose pinky-sized pallid grubs are not as attractive as they sound. Despite our best efforts to keep them from our cattle's feed, flies still harassed the livestock and planted larvae, and those larvae developed into grubs under the cowhide. Besides the cosmetic flaw, grubs also created "jellied beef" around the encysted area. There is no upside to jellied beef. The grubs had to be removed.

I had a system. Standard procedure was to scrape off the top of the cyst and use one's fingers to squeeze the grub out through the cow's thick hide—a process as difficult as it is nasty, and which invites the steer to kick in disapproval. I discovered instead that I could invert a Coke bottle onto a scraped cyst and, with a hefty push downward, see the grub shoot up into the bottle.

You pop enough grubs and you win. I did.

———

I worked on the ranch because I had to. I showed cattle because I was expected to. I danced because I needed to.

By age five I had hectored my mom and Grandma Susie into ferrying me to the tiny ballet studio that was Granby's only dance school. Soon I showed enough promise that my mother drove me three hours to Denver every Saturday, where I could take classes in tap, ballet, jazz, and acrobatics, enough to develop a solid foundation in each. But I wanted more, and my mom, never content with our small-town barriers, wanted to find that for me.

Then I discovered gymnastics, under the tutelage of Rod Hill, husband-coach to Debbie Hill, third-ranked in the nation and Olympic teammate of Cathy Rigby. Three days a week our new schedule was: out of school at three, at the gym from six to nine, home by midnight. My mom drove and smoked. I did homework and slept. We bonded this way for years, as I began to succeed in regional meets.

I plotted my life's arc, even while my grandfather, father, ranch hands, and classmates ridiculed the study. "You're going to jump around and play for a living? How is that honest work?"

I didn't fit in.

———

In addition to being my gymnastics chauffeur, and as part of her efforts to demonstrate that the world was bigger than the fence-lines around our ranch, my mother arranged culture days, trips to Denver for me and any brother not ranching or rodeoing. The event corresponding with the start of my sophomore year at West Grand High School brought us to Red Rocks Amphitheatre, a natural sandstone soundscape overlooking Denver. My father and brother Clair, two years older, joined us.

Performing that night was Up With People, dozens of cheerful and sincere teenagers, singing promise for America with titles like "Freedom Isn't Free" and "What Color Is God's Skin?" Cynical counterculture types or sheltered city folk might recoil at the earnestness and overt patriotism, each dance practically a group salute. Not me. Not Clair. We loved the Americana and the red sweaters, the Pat-Boone pop sound, the enthusiasm and pride. And when they sang, "Colorado," about rugged, bold folks at the great Continental Divide, we knew they were singing to us.

The show concluded by announcing that Up With People, the same organization that would play four Super Bowl halftime shows and perform with Bob Hope at the Nixon White House, was sponsoring local groups—*Sing Out* groups—to share this same message and sing these same songs. The performers invited the crowd to start their own.

Clair and I now had a mission. Suddenly we could do something about the moral decay we saw on television. We could make a difference with the youth of the country. We could counterbalance the destructive, narcissistic, free-love hedonism and wasted lives disintegrating around us.

We could sing a jaunty tune.

This was 1970. Sing Out Colorado Springs had formed the year before, and Clair and I reached out to them, arranging for their troupe to perform in Kremmling. Part of the Sing Out culture included having its students stay at sponsor homes when they toured. We opened our house; so did our Kremmling neighbors.

Among the performers staying in my neighborhood was Gary Simpson, the first black American I had ever seen. Among the performers staying in my house was Rachel Legg (née Brown), who would become one of my dearest, lifelong friends.

Following their model, and with the help of our West Grand High School music teacher, Clair and I strove to copy the success of Sing Out Colorado Springs. We planted posters across town: "Come ride with Paul Revere. Come ride with Sing Out West Grand." They worked.

The Sing Out West Grand group grew to three dozen strong, and performed through spring and summer at fairs, at high schools, at the Cattleman's Convention, and on street corners. The choreography was mine, the songs were from Up With People, and the enthusiasm and heartfelt reception from host families was universal.

Elsewhere in Colorado, Gary Simpson and Sing Out Colorado Springs found a similar reception. He told me so in the letters he sent. I wrote back expressing my delight at the difference we were making in our communities, and how much fun I was having. He replied telling me how funny I was, and that I made him smile. I sent back jokes and school news, and remembered his dark skin.

This went on.

My brother and I traveled the state with our high school group, sometimes literally singing for our supper, but back at home we still had ranch work to do.

On my Grandpa Ted Orr's ranch, between Granby and Kremmling, the Colorado River cut a picture-postcard vista as it irrigated the natural Timothy grass meadows—meadows I was haying in August of 1971. Two days prior, the grass had been cut with the sickle mower; now it was dry enough to rake into windrows. Two days hence I'd be back again on the tractor to sweep the windrows in front of the stacker, all part of the essential and time-sensitive summer drill that kept our cattle fed and our crews busy from the moment the dew dried to past sundown.

Just before noon Grandpa Ted drove up. From the side of his mouth, around the toothpick and leaning out his pickup window, my father's father said, "There's three guys waiting to see you." He bit hard on the tiny piece of wood. "Back at the house. Get in."

It was hot on the tractor, hotter in Ted's truck. He was seething: hunched more than usual over the steering wheel, rough old hands yanking the pickup to heel over dirt roads and tractor ruts, his welder's squint in full squeeze.

Nobody visits in the middle of a ranch workday. Too much to do. Too far to travel.

At the house Grandpa posted himself sentry: hands perched on his potbelly, in greasy overalls and a scowl. Boots curled up and hat curled down.

I said hello to Gary Simpson.

"Hi, Val!" Gary's huge smile was all white teeth and pride. "Surprised? Phil and Bob and I just decided to drive up and see you! It's been months."

That would have been three months prior, when on a lark I had corralled two friends to drive with me to surprise Gary at a regional track meet. He had been third in the two-mile run, and just as surprised to see me then as I was now. Grandpa Ted and everyone else in my family knew about my road trip to cheer for a friend, but none of them had actually seen Gary.

Grandpa Ted hadn't moved. His eyes were in shadow but his hat stayed pointed at Gary.

"I don't even know what to say," I said. "You three drove four hours up here just to say, 'Hi'?"

Gary beamed. Ted spit out the toothpick. Bob looked questions at me. Phil started to shuffle.

"Guys, it's really good to see you," I said. I could tell that my grandfather needed me back on that tractor. "But I have to work. This is just not a good time to visit."

"That's no problem," said Gary. "We can wait until you get off." Phil laid his hand on his friend's elbow and tilted his head towards the door.

"It'll be past dark," I said. "We're haying." My grandpa's posture seemed off kilter, almost as if his squat, thickset frame were tensing to spring. But these boys were no danger: they were my friends.

Ted said nothing.

Phil took charge. "Let's leave Val to her work, Gary. We should pick a less busy day for her."

Once I had seen the boys off, Grandpa Ted finally spoke. "Who are they?"

"Gary's my friend from Sing Out. From Colorado Springs." I was now looking directly at my grandfather and still could not read his face.

"This Bob and Phil. One of them your boyfriend?"

Of course. Grandpa Ted was being protective of his sixteen-year-old granddaughter, especially within the rough male confines of a working ranch. "Grandpa, no. They're just Gary's friends. I've been writing to Gary for months. You remember—I went to see him race. He's sweet." Gary was sweet. He was also funny and charming and shy and strong and fast.

"You will not."

I didn't follow.

"How will this look?" Forceful spittle colored his question. "Gary's black. What will the townsfolk say?"

What will the townsfolk say?

"We don't have black people in Kremmling." Grandpa seldom said so many words in a row, and never with such a rising ferocity. "Why are you hanging out with people like this?"

People like this?

His lips drawn back and his eyes full of disgust, my grandfather made every word a commandment: "You will not have a nigger friend. You will not!"

"oh." The tiniest sound came out, as I understood.

I understood why he had been so angry. I understood in an instant that my elders were not always right, but instead could be impossibly, utterly wrong. I understood the ugliness of a racism so intimate that I could see it in the flare of this crusty old man's nostrils.

I understood that Ted and I would never be close again, and every word that followed included my tears to prove it. *I miss you already, Grandpa.*

"But I will."

I felt my shoulders rise and my breath come deeply. "I will write to him. They are my friends and they will remain my friends." This person defying Ted, this pixie-haired, sunburnt girl in 501 Levi's, the one whose force of will staked her insubordinate claim out loud—she was new to the world, planting her boots squarely in ranch dirt to make her first stand. But her beliefs were lifelong, echoing Grandma Susie's simple truth that we are all the same inside, reflecting Grandpa Ed's mantra that it's how you treat people every day that matters, recognizing that skin color would never be a reason to treat someone differently.

"I will write to him." Simple, certain truth, proven out over the following months, over the objections of Ted, my parents, and the narrow, soda-straw community who would hear from my grandfather how a black boy came to town one day. "Now take me back to the tractor. I have work to do."

———

At over nine thousand feet above sea level, remote Strawberry Lake, a scenic twenty minutes northeast of Granby, teeters on the Continental Divide. Sportfishers prefer the nearby reservoir of Lake Granby for its mackinaw trout and kokanee salmon, but on footpaths beyond the reservoir's last gas stations and boat docks, adventurous hikers can discover Strawberry Lake's adjacent meadow, expansive enough to support elk, black bear, cougar, and mule deer.

Or hippies.

Just not twenty thousand of them.

The first North American Rainbow Gathering, the Woodstock of the West, convened in July, 1972 to "pray for peace and a change in the world." When the influx into Arapaho National Forest first overloaded local services, state police tried to block the access road. When thousands more arrived the next day, Colorado Governor John Love called in the National Guard to establish heavy roadblocks. A deluge of tie-dyed humanity trudging around the barricades to hike four miles uphill finally forced the Governor and Forest Service to relent and grant a "one-time" exemption for such a sizable gathering on National Forest land. Forty years later, in whichever state the Rainbow Gathering selects for its July event, the Forest Service continues to grant one-time exemptions.

Down the hill, in Granby proper, I sold crisp plaid shirts with shiny snaps, and pointy-toed boots.

Mornings in the summer between my junior and senior years at Kremmling High were still devoted to ranch work, but I wanted something different. The Trading Post, a western-clothing store, offered that. Retail work was tidily shelved and clean, and the clientele were usually clean, too. Until the hippies.

"What's *that* about?" Store owner Francis Jenkins grimaced like he'd entered an outhouse by mistake. I heard our store door's bell jingle, and turned from the hat section ("Felt, straw, or leather?") to see a flower child step inside.

Our Granby sidewalks had become holding pens for the Rainbow Gathering spillover, and often hippies would slip from them into storefronts to cool off, quiet down, or fill their pockets. We were obliged to be vigilant, to keep our eyes on the "customers." This one commanded more than casual attention. It wasn't so much the matted hair or the unlaundered sack dress or the mud-caked feet. It was the necklace.

Real garlic and onion in an elaborate braid around her neck—and not fresh. Not at all fresh.

It fell to the proprietor to approach and attend the customer. Francis, the wholesale cowboy, asked her, "What's the point—?" He circled a hand in front of his chest as if oiling an invisible saddle. Or holding her at bay. He also kept his breath shallow.

"These . . ." She presented her allium jewelry with a flourish, "are to ward off the evil spirits." She surveyed the cowboy offerings inside our trading post and apparently saw nothing to match her ensemble. "They keep away anything bad that might happen to me."

"Yeah," I said, from a safe distance. "Because nobody wants to get close enough to you to do anything."

She was already gone.

For the past two years I'd been wearing fringed red, white, and blue and singing "The World Is My Hometown" with the Sing Out West Grand group. I'd been wearing my cheerleader's purple and gold to spur the Mustangs to victory. I'd been wearing dirt-brown riding gear to move cattle all summer.

But at least I'd been wearing clothes.

A day later, Onion-Girl's moneyed soul sister stepped into the Trading Post, cash in hand, with a purpose. I was working boots ("Standard, Western, or ropers?"), and motioned her over. Francis joined us. Hardworking, good-ol'-boy, straight-laced Francis. "Rainbow" needed bib overalls. While I was finishing a boot sale, Francis and I both eyed her, up and down, for sizing. A good close look. We agreed that Rainbow was a 32" waist, 36" chest, and 28" inseam.

"I'll go get them," he said. Our stock was in the back room, well past the belts and buckles, two aisles over from dishware and pottery, and out of sight of boots. Far enough away that Rainbow had time to get ready to try on her imminent purchase. By removing every stitch. In the boot department.

The boot department does not have a dressing room.

Francis spun back around the corner, overalls in hand, only to cartoon-halt dead in his tracks. It seemed he was about to tell her that he had found the exact size, but even though his jaw worked as if he were talking, no sounds came forth.

Buck-naked Rainbow was happy to try on her new bib overalls, and to discover a perfect fit. She beamed and modeled a wobbly pirouette, just to make sure.

Francis finally got some words out. "You can just have them."

Thousands of hippies overstayed the July 4 song circles and prayer moots, littering Granby and squatting on surrounding ranches for months. It seemed they missed the vans leaving town, even though the bumper-sticker fare of "gas, grass, or ass" was clearly marked.

Hippies got dirtier as July got hotter. So did their children. The only grocery store in town, Mr. Ed's Food Market, was adjacent to the Trading Post. Leaving work one evening I stepped around a cluster of free spirits—maybe it was a family—sitting curbside between our two establishments, eating.

At their side, half-empty, was a bag of large-breed dog food. Hands dipped into the bag, some large, some small. Crunching sounds, some loud, some quiet.

I couldn't help myself. "Why are you eating *that*?"

The eldest, perhaps thirty years old, pointed to the brand name. "We tried 'em all," he said, dispensing bohemian wisdom, "and Chuck Wagon's the best."

Disgusted, I looked into Mr. Ed's to see the cashier shrug. What kind of surreal America had descended upon my little cotton cocoon? In my town children don't eat dog food. In my town we don't have hitchhikers everywhere, dogs running loose, crowds in filthy clothes, kids eating ice cream off the sidewalk, women half-dressed, and so much unkempt, nasty hair, always long.

In my house people can't even grow their own hair long, not according to Jack Orr. "You can grow your hair long if you want to," Dad would say, "But by God you're not going to live here." Who is setting rules in this extended commune? Who is taking care of things? If this is what follows from drugs and sex and rock and roll, then I want no part of it.

But neither did I want any more of being the reluctant cattle queen.

I had just won Senior Champion in Showmanship at the Colorado State Fair, for being the best, statewide, at properly showing a steer. The prior year I showed the Reserve Champion Hereford. The year before that I was Junior State Champion in Showmanship. There were more, a closetful more, of dusty satin curlicued ribbons attesting to my years as Orr showgirl.

Seeing me lead my steer from the show ring after the Senior Champion announcement, halter strap in my right hand (exactly eight inches from the steer's head), dress show-stick in my left (pointed down for etiquette), my older cousin Mitch hustled alongside. The girl my dad called "a hell of a hand on the ranch," because I didn't live up to his standards, had to make sure.

"Val, tell me you've changed your mind," she said. "You won. This is as good as it gets."

Nothing had changed since my news to the family just before the fair. "That's the point. I'm done. This is my last year of showing cattle."

She looked around the arena and bleachers, taking in the sea of hats, the dust, and the pervasive bellow and tang of hundreds of cattle on the hoof. "I cannot believe that you are giving all this up."

I heard the clang of pens, and the restless animals within.
"Yeah, I really am."

———

From the time we moved the thirty miles from Granby to Kremmling I had felt out of place. Ever since arriving halfway through first grade, in the middle of winter, with all of my new classmates already "friended up," I knew I didn't belong.

I traveled to Phoenix and Los Angeles and Kansas City for cattle shows, to Alamosa and Mesa Verde to sing America's virtues, and to Denver for backflips and the balance beam. Kremmling people didn't do any of that. And even though I was a cheerleader for Kremmling's West Grand High School, I spent much of my time with my Granby friends, their cross-county rivals, at the cost of cold shoulders and shouts of "traitor!" I spent school years in small-minded Kremmling and summers ranching in do-as-you're-told Granby, without a sense of belonging in either. I had fallen in love with a black boy in a whites-only town. And I walked away from the cattle life.

There was a bigger world out there, one beyond the dust and leather, beyond the creosote and manure and grubs. But one without drugs and destitution. Without dog food for dinner or shameless nudity. One with theater and dignity and prosperity and culture and ballet and majesty and clean fingernails.

And it was mine to find.

With Ted, age two, and Kendra, age one, just after escaping from Mike

CHAPTER SIX

Where There's Smoke

"I want you to know. I have just hit your daughter."

FIRST HUSBAND, MIKE CUNNINGHAM

On a hot August night in 1978, one month before I got pregnant with my first child, I took a black eye from that baby's father.

Mike worked the Eisenhower Tunnel near Empire, Colorado, on its second bore through the granite and gneiss of the Rocky Mountains. At the time the highest vehicular tunnel in the world, it carried Interstate 70 underneath the Continental Divide at Loveland Pass. At nearby Peaceful Valley Trailer Park, on the harvest-gold appliances of our cramped single-wide, I had prepared another dinner of kokanee fish, our staple for the previous month. Absent money, Outdoorsman Mike provided for us with his rifle and fishing pole, and the season's bounty from Dillon Reservoir was kokanee, freshwater sockeye salmon on whose steady diet we thrived over the summer.

The salmon had long since cooled on our plates, three glasses of iced tea and four loads of laundry ago.

Mike trudged in from around the corner, heavy king-of-the-castle footsteps. Five strides to the kitchen—each one shook our trailer's flimsy chassis—to loom dust-black against gold linoleum, the stench of smoke and stale beer revealing, again, why he was hours late. Over the previous weeks his after-work drinks with the guys had stretched into the late evenings, a habit I felt betrayed our newlywed status. "It's rude to not at least call me. I've had dinner ready."

"Get off my case," he slurred. "I work hard."

I stepped close. "Knock it off! You work dangerous." Six people were to die during the second tunnel's construction; three had died during the first. "I never know if you're okay when—"

Two hands against my chest. His dirt-ringed eyes. A sudden shove.

He had pushed me before, a little, but never so cold. I realized I was flat on my back on the floor, that my head had just bounced off the linoleum. He straddled me in a playground bully's position.

I had tussled with my brothers growing up. We wrestled, knocked down, piled on, and hollered "Uncle." I held my own then. This was different, and very wrong.

Mike Cunningham balled up his workman's fist, raised it high, and slammed it into my left eye. He was yelling now: "Shut up!" He slapped me full across the face. "I do *not* answer to anybody. Not a wife. Not anybody!"

This is not happening. I'm not an abused woman; this happens to other women. I don't get hit.

But I knew that the black eye I was about to wear would reveal that I do get hit, that a wedding ring was no protection from a mean drunk.

I tried to shove him off, but he was too heavy and too loud. More from frustration than hurt—the shock blunted the immediate pain—I started to cry, a language that found momentary purchase. He got off me, his dominance proven, his breath short.

I rose with a hand on our flea-market kitchen table, and pushed past him and past our makeshift sofa and our dirty gold carpet and our Salvation-Army stereo. The stereo on whose cabinet I had displayed a recent treasure: a wedding gift presenting our invitation, laminated with flowers and the midnight blue of our ceremony, a beautiful, sentimental gift adjacent to our engagement photo: him casual, me fresh.

Once in the master bedroom, I just sobbed. Uncontrolled, heaving waves of disbelief and fear. Of guilt and regret. Of the inevitability of this pattern, knowing that I had brought this on myself.

They said I shouldn't marry him, but I had given my word. Jack Orr's first principle: "Your word is your bond. You say you're going to do something, by God, you do it!" Yes, Dad.

Then: *Cling-dangk!* Our broken doorbell, followed by a providential voice outside, my mother's. Mike's composure regained, he paced his words carefully. Through the door I heard, "I want you to know. I have just hit your daughter."

I would not face my mom when she entered the bedroom, keeping my head buried in a pillow so she couldn't see my face. I was still sobbing.

"Well," she said to my back as I lay face down on my bed. "Did you deserve it?"

Did I? They had all been correct—everyone who said I shouldn't have married him, and I ignored every sign. The wallet photo of his high-school girlfriend, the sudden pockets full of convenience-store trinkets he flashed, his slaughtering dozens of off-season elk in one day, the surprise of finding Alice-in-Wonderland mushrooms being cultivated under my bed, his bloody manner of meting out barroom justice, and story after story of his next big job.

A week before the wedding I had called my dearest friends Rachel and Squid and Nona for nearly identical conversations.

Me: "What the hell am I doing? This is wrong."

Her: "You need to call the wedding off."

Me: "I gave my word. I said I'd marry him, so I have to do this."

Her: "Don't do it."

Me: "I have four hundred people coming and I can't say no."

Every instinct said I needed to not marry Mike Cunningham, but every lesson I'd been taught said to follow through with what I started. I had not yet learned to trust my instincts.

————

Mun-roe, *Loozy*-ana—America's 6th poorest city, and mostly black. Apathetic poor. Street-corner poor. Dirt-floor poor. A sad, bayou poverty I'd never seen before, one that crossed color lines and tied both black and white to their Jim Crow upbringing. Monroe lived in the past.

I had just arrived in this foreign land by plane, two mewling infants in tow, to find that Mike's claim of having an oil-rig job when he drove out two weeks earlier from Colorado was a lie. I also soon discovered that he hadn't quit his previous job, but instead had been fired for stealing the Coors beer he was supposed to be delivering.

"I got the sunofabitch." I heard him tell California Bob over the phone, regarding the boss who fired him from Coors. "Thinks he owns me, but I don't need his piss-ass job. Let's see how his fancy Jeep runs on Karo syrup."

There was no work in Louisiana, not that the roach-infested duplex he had rented for us called for much of a wage. But Mike had no job at all, despite his days-long absences and stories of working a rig off the Gulf coast. Plenty of stories. No paychecks.

The little money I arrived with ran out fast. I sold our furniture. I sold Lupi, our trained retrieving dog. And I discovered "southern hospitality." I did not like it.

One day at a no-name convenience store I gathered up bread, rice, and diapers, and while heading to the back of the line calculated that I'd have three dollars remaining for gas, enough for two days, no more. The clerk caught my attention and waved me up.

"It's fine," I said. "I'll wait my turn."

She was white.

It took me a moment to register that everyone in front of me was black.

"No. You need to c'mon up here now," she said, this time with intent. The people in front of me began a familiar shuffle to make way.

The Civil War is still going on down here!

"No, ma'am. I *will* wait my turn." And I did, under her harsh glare and behind an uncomfortable queue.

I hate this place. I hate this narrow-minded, oblivious contempt.

I hated our infested duplex in a squalid section of a dirty town. I hated that my babies were so far from their family. I hated the swamp-and-diesel stench that would not wash clean.

But I did love the black churches. I attended for the solace, and discovered the music. I heard full-throated, unabashed worship, celebrations straight from man to God, earnest and guilt-free, with no earth-bound racial taint. In the black churches I saw pure, sincere humanity expressing faith in uplifted song, smiles welcoming my Colorado winter-pale skin right alongside the blackest great-grandchild of a slave.

That harmony was not universal.

A month into our stay I woke to amber and scarlet flickers above me, where our ceiling usually showed only plaster cracks and water stains. Our red-brick unit comprised a back bedroom, where babies Ted and Kendra slept, a single dingy bathroom off the living and kitchen area, and my bedroom, streetside. Through its window I saw the fire.

Across the street, the lawn sloped up to my neighbors' tiny house. I didn't know them—I didn't know any of my neighbors—but I knew their skin color.

I saw the fire. The cross was nearly the house's height, planted at the top of the slope, where anyone inside could feel the heat and hear the spit and crackle.

I saw the fire. The same shape as in the church, but opposite its message, a vivid orange middle-of-night ugliness. Open-jawed, I gripped the window frame with both hands, steadying myself from the disbelief, the fear, the rising nausea, the sudden punch-in-the-gut sickness.

I saw the fire, its flames now lighting adjacent houses, enough to see figures dart back inside other rooms like mine, leaving curtains swinging behind them. If they don't look, they can tell themselves that a cross is not burning right where they live. I was now trembling with too much anger to step away. This was terrorism in my America, and it was utterly, maddeningly, infuriatingly wrong. What kind of America had we fallen into?

I looked for the bleached hoods and robes. The Ku Klux Klan was out there, replaying with blazing color the hatred I'd seen only in grainy black and white on my parent's tiny set almost twenty years ago. But this Klan skulked around corners and melted into shadows and evaded my search.

———

My friend Ed Jones, a past Colorado State Senator, describes his upbringing in Mississippi in the 1940s, a decade and state where he, a black youth, needed to get off the sidewalk, eyes down, should any white person approach. Every Saturday morning, after making breakfast for a white dentist while Ed waited on the back stoop, his mother walked him downtown.

"I want you to watch something," she said. At 9 a.m. sharp, the college-educated teacher and cook sat alongside her negro boy on the Main Street curb. This time each week signaled the march of the KKK through the center of town, decked in their floor-length, solid-white robes—but without the pointed hoods.

"Why don't they wear their hoods?" Ed asked.

"They want you to know what your place is in the world."

And while these 1980s Louisiana Klansmen weren't as brazen as their 1940s Mississippi counterparts, their tactics of intimidation were no less vile.

Getting closer was out of the question, with Mike "on assignment" and two babies asleep, but I looked for this Klan. I looked for them behind tomorrow's "How do, Ma'am?" and next week's "C'mon up to the front of the line."

They were not hard to find.

———

Two months later, in the boondocks of Loleta in northern California, I decided I needed more getaway money.

Chasing work, Mike had uprooted us from our brief Louisiana sojourn. California Bob's promise of a cement job, and the presence of Mike's brother and sister-in-law settled our fate. We stayed with Ken and Becky for seven weeks, long enough for me to know that Ken was his brother's eyes when Mike was away for work; long enough to learn that Stephanie, Mike's wallet-photo high-school girlfriend, lived in town; and long enough to realize that abuse in the Cunningham family tree was about to continue.

Since leaving Monroe, I had been able to scratch together one hundred dollars, carried nowhere except my back pocket, since Mike always rifled through my possessions. I was working on two hundred more, piecemeal, from brief shopping excursions that included skimming what I could. Those errands granted my only solitude, and I used them to steal the occasional payphone call to my mom, in which we planned my escape.

Mike's cement job became a fishing job near San Francisco, 250 miles south, slated to start the following week. He was home for the weekend, the California surf and sunset our entertainment.

"You know, Mike," I said. "Maybe the kids and I ought to just go back to Colorado for a while. Just until you get settled down and get the right job and make enough money to get our own place. Maybe that would be a good thing."

"You can go—but those kids are never going." As calm and relentless as the tide.

Within twenty-four hours I told North American Van Lines, Alta Orr, and the local sheriff my departure date and time: Thursday next, 8:00 a.m.

On April 24, 1981, Mike headed south at midnight. Before dawn I began separating our things, quietly so that Ted and Kendra could sleep, but not quietly enough. Ken blocked the hall, arms crossed. "You're leaving us today, aren't you?"

Ken's squint and set jaw revealed his fraternal loyalty. I weighed my meager options. Chose truth. "Yes, I am." I knew also that my mom had planned to fly into Redding the day prior, and drive the three hours west to join me, but I had no way to verify that she was on the way. Likewise, Ken had no way to reach Mike, by now at sea. "And the police will be here and a moving van."

Ken calculated, and then stepped aside.

When my mom arrived I put my children into her arms. "Take Ted and Kendra," I said. "If anything goes down, you get in that car and get those kids out of here. I will find my way back to Colorado." Three hundred in my hip pocket would be enough.

Movers and police arrived on time.

Four days later, at my parents' house in Golden, Colorado, the phone rang at 4:44 a.m.—Mike, telling me he's in Las Vegas with Stephanie. When the courthouse opened I was first in line, filing for divorce and a restraining order.

———

Mike Cunningham was a backwoods con man with a hair-trigger, always itching for a fight. He fought for sport and for twisted hillbilly dominance. He stole to show cunning, and swindled with a devil-may-care grin. He was a reckless drunk and as dangerous, remorseless, and pretty as a bobcat.

But he wasn't angry.

The Angry White Male came later.

Marble plaques I had made for the legal team

Angry White Male

"Our first game is called 'well begun is half done.'"

MARY POPPINS

"There's another job we lost for being white," said Randy. "The San Juan National Forest one. Same as before, we had the low bid."

"Who to this time?" It didn't matter; I knew the list. Of the five subcontractors for guardrail construction in Colorado, ours was the only not designated a minority- or woman-owned firm. The other four got preference.

"Gonzalez. And they overbid us by seventeen hundred dollars. Seventeen—" he choked on the silence where an expletive belonged, but Randy didn't swear. Didn't drink or stray either. He had other vices.

He had been complaining about the unfairness of losing jobs this way throughout the 80s, of getting passed over because of our skin color, gender, and nationality. Government transportation projects included bonuses for a prime contractor who doled at least a ten percent quota of the work to firms designated as DBEs, disadvantaged business enterprises. "Disadvantaged" for this purpose meant nothing more than being majority-owned by women or someone of certain racial classifications; the disadvantage was presumed and did not have to be demonstrated. From the contract bonus, a prime could afford to be generous with a little DBE lagniappe.

Our family business was the one in Colorado that got none of those set-asides, even though we were woman-owned. I held 62% of the company stock, but we were in no way disadvantaged because of it. We ran a strong company, held an impeccable reputation for quality work, and earned our success, every dollar. I wasn't about to adopt some misleading label to suggest otherwise, despite Randy's penchant to play along. All I wanted to do was get my boots on and get my feet on the ground and go do our job—labels be damned. On the ranch no one handed me a pink cowboy hat and said, "Val doesn't have to work." Same here. Let's just go put up some rail.

He started up again. "Half those companies are fronts anyway. Everybody knows it. It's not right."

"Same old story, Randy. So what are you going to do about it?"

"We needed this job," he said. "I got two dozen men to keep busy."

"That's enough! I'm tired of hearing you keep complaining," I said. "We may as well accept discrimination as the way this business works, or—"

"It's not right." Randy picked only those fights he could win, only unfair fights, but against bigger obstacles he slunk and pouted.

"Or . . . we decide we're going to do something about it and change the law. Change it or shut up. It's time we decided. Which one?"

"It's not right." He was spent. No more answers. No change.

It wasn't right that our own government was treating businesses differently because of their owners' race and gender. It had to be fixed. As a woman I wanted to earn a job because I had the best quality at the lowest price, not because of my gender. What an insult to imagine getting work because the government viewed me as less competent, as needing a handout of taxpayer dollars and a pat on the head like some second-class business. If I couldn't compete without donations, then maybe I needed to pick another industry.

I chose to fight. In the face of such bias I had to take action, although I had no idea where to start, and no inkling that this pursuit of fairness would encompass fifteen years and three Supreme Court appearances.

Ranch history told me that when you made your mind up on something, you acted. Be decisive. Occasionally that showed up as impulsive, like reconnecting with an old college pal after escaping from Loleta, California six years prior. Randy had been a friend for years, and when I returned to Colorado I remembered his all-American-boy manners and clear moral code and exceptionally tight family attachments. Within eight months after leaving Mike Cunningham I married Randy Pech. Impulses have consequences.

I married into the family business, one Randy started with his father and a family friend, Tom Adams (his name was the source for the first half of "Adarand," Randy's the second). His father and Tom had left in the late 70s, leaving Randy as solo proprietor, and me, soon after, as working partner. As the business grew through the 80s, Randy chose to transfer more and more of its ownership to me: he brought documents for my signature. I trusted and signed. He knew best about business matters, and to me, as long as the ownership remained within the family I saw no harm.

Who can you trust if not family?

———

Jack Orr shook the snow off his long white beard and then handed it to me.

He grinned his grandpa grin. "They like it?" He peeled off the red stocking cap and set to unbuttoning the bowl-full-of-jelly jacket.

"They're asking, 'Where's the reindeer?'" I said. "Mom's upstairs telling them that Rudolph is taking a break, and Ski-dolph is filling in."

We could still hear the scurry and titters of six pajamaed cousins, my Ted and Kendra among them, dashing from window to window for any late glimpses of the snowmobiling Santa who had just buzzed our Granby ranch house.

Ungloved, Jack's hands gave off a Christmas Eve chill. I took them in mine, rubbing for warmth. My father's hands were less callused than when he was only ranching, and smaller than I remembered. Real estate and political forays had softened the hide and healed the rope burns.

"Let's get up there before they miss me," he said, playful cheer still flush on wind-burnt cheeks. "Those kids are pretty clever." He made no move to get up.

Let's not. I have thirty years of catching up to do in this moment.

Later, with children all deep in sugar-plum slumber, Randy and I sat with Jack over eggnog—heavy on the nog. None for Randy, of course. He had ice cream after his Christmas dinner. Randy was always happier after dinner, and especially happier after ice cream. Over the years I made sure he got plenty of ice cream.

"So how's business?" Dad asked. The tinsel-rush over, he was back to commerce. He looked at me, but Randy answered.

"It's getting worse. Being low bid any more isn't good enough. You got to be Hispanic, too."

"I don't get it with you two. Sounds like you still got lots of jobs," Jack said. "You're busy all the time for as often as you drop off the kids here. Seems there's plenty of work to go around."

Christmas at the ranch: Santa Jack with Ted, Kendra, and cousins

We were busy. We won more guardrail jobs than any other Colorado subcontractor. But it wasn't only about the work; it was about the principle. At its core, the practice of using race to mete out taxpayer-funded bribes was fundamentally anti-American and wrong.

Jack Orr was a cattleman. I tried using that angle to make the point. "Okay, Dad, it's like we're taking our feeder calves to auction and our Hispanic neighbor is taking his to the same auction. Come sale time, he's going to get ten cents more on the hoof than we do just because he's Hispanic. No other reason."

"Well, that would be wrong."

"Bingo! That's exactly what's happening," I said. "We're not being judged on our work. We're being judged on our last name and our skin color and our gender and what country we came from. There aren't any preferences for the great-granddaughter of a Colorado homesteader. But be from Africa or Central America . . ."

My Dad's patience and eggnog mug were empty. "Why you keep going on about it, then? You do something about it or you shut up."

"I've been trying. I called the EEOC office. We were at state highway commission hearings. I talked to folks at the Department of Transportation and offered to help set up an emerging business program. I wrote letters to Congressman Hefley. I even talked to highway departments in other states to see how they handle it."

"And?" He refilled his mug from the Cutty Sark bottle.

"A little sympathy. No help. They mostly say 'play the game.' Turns out it's a national problem, too big for one person to stand up to." Especially one person whose husband's tolerance for conflict ends when the first adult fights back.

My dad took a good long holiday swig, savoring the bite. Inviting the numbness.

"There's some folks I think you ought to talk to."

———

These folks were Mountain States Legal Foundation, a Denver-based public interest law firm championing individual liberty, property rights, and free enterprise, a group to which my father had been contributing for years.

We met first with Todd Welch, an attorney whose small-town Wyoming roots fostered an early rapport. He and I had spoken on the phone enough for him to understand our business and the circumstances. Now he had to vet us in person. After introductions, he led us to Mountain States' conference room, where a mile-high panorama filled the twenty-third-floor window. "Most of our clients don't get to see this. They usually live too far away to visit our office," he said. Randy turned away, white and shaken; he hated heights.

The attorney wasted no time. "We're behind closed doors now, just the three of us. Whatever you say to me is privileged. Utterly protected. You understand that?

We nodded.

"Okay then. What's your price?"

"I don't follow," I said.

"You've lost profits. Tens of thousands, maybe hundreds of thousands. What will it take to make you whole? To be done with all this?"

"It's not about the money."

Todd pressed. "Sure it is. When we find a case of yours and start pushing it through the courts, at some point two years from now the feds are going to offer a giant contract or a certain sum to wrap this up, and that amount could be sizable. Let's establish that figure up front, just between us, confidentially. To know where we stand."

I had thought we were on the same side, but I was becoming less sure. "It's not about *any* amount of money. It's about changing the law." If I had to plead my own case to my own lawyers, I would. "It's about doing what's right. It's about regaining freedom of opportunity and it's about changing the laws of the land. It's about what is right for our nation, not just us."

"Of course it is," said Todd, seeing me pass the test. "Let me introduce you to our president."

William Perry Pendley, Esquire, Chief Legal Officer for MSLF, would become the public face of the cause, and properly so. With his commanding height, impeccable attire and coif, and Wyatt Earp mustache, he leant authentic western gravitas to what would become a national case.

But first we needed just the right one.

Over the next few months, I met several times with Todd and Perry, reviewing Adarand's lost contracts, the legal precedents standing in our way, and the fortitude that Randy and I would have to evince to make our case a good match for Mountain States. I usually had to visit the law office alone; Randy's fear of the elevator kept him home. I didn't mind.

Perry charted our course with clarity. "I'm asking a lot," he said. "I'm asking you to stay with us for the long haul, because our objective is not to settle. If you want money, find the lawyers who want to sue and get something. But if you want to change the law, if you think this is wrong and you want to get this turned around, then we're your guys.

"It's going to get tough. The odds are we'll lose at the district court, we'll lose at the court of appeals, and the Supreme Court will decide not to hear the case and it'll go away. Within two years, it'll be over, with nothing to show."

I set my jaw. Ok then, that's the way it will be.

"But knock on wood. We may get a ruling." Perry's voice crunched like an old gravel road, and promised the same guidance. I would go where it led.

I felt generations of frontier steel and resolve, a family history of Colorado homesteaders willing to stake their fortunes on fencelines and principle, drawing lines that mattered in places others wouldn't.

"All I want to do is change the law."

Now if only I could change my husband.

———

The long struggle that was to come in the courthouse was not the hardest battle I had to fight. At home, the Angry White Male began to reveal himself.

It started with a sulk, a shout, a clatter, and a slam.

Earlier that day, Randy and Ted had trekked to the hardware store for dowels, balsa planks, and glue, the first step in building the log cabin that was my son's weekend elementary-school project. A simple log cabin from scratch, the assignment said. No Lincoln Logs. Parents are specifically asked to assist, it went on, but the cabin must be the student's work. I was just pleased that Randy made time for his son. He had adopted both children shortly after we were married, but too seldom found time for either, given the work demands of Adarand.

Before leaving, Ted wrapped his arms around my neck, kissed me goodbye, and whispered, "I get to use a drill and a saw when we get back. Dad said so." He struggled to pronounce his esses around two missing incisors.

"Make it just like my first house," I whispered back. Ted liked hearing the story of how I lived in a log cabin until I was eight months old; he had seen the pictures. The house was so tiny, I had often told him, that instead of a crib I slept in a dresser drawer they pulled open at night. It was true, as far as I knew.

Shortly, whirrs and zings from the garage announced their progress. I heard more electric whines than I might have predicted, given the small scale of the project, but teaching your son the nuances of power tools likely took numerous demonstrations, and based on the hours they were spending, Ted was surely receiving thorough instruction.

"Get it right!"

I heard the shout from upstairs, Randy's unchecked, fed-up voice carrying through two walls. On my way down the stairs, I heard the clatter, an eruption of wood-block cacophony and hailstorm pings. At the bottom of the stairs I saw and felt the door slam as Randy thundered into the house, face scarlet and both fists clenched. My choice was to step aside and get to Ted or to invite a confrontation. I picked correctly, and let him pass.

My little boy was on his knees, collecting splintered logs. I joined him. We found pieces under the car, scattered across the countertop, and at the far corner from the workbench where the remainder of the project frame still jutted. Hands full of miniature timber, we wordlessly deposited the beams and slats, some wet with white glue, into a pile near the tools, carefully sorting the logs by length and notch pattern, broken and unbroken.

At the workbench the cabin's inverted carcass remained. Randy had created some type of custom form, a four-post scaffolding inside which he had been assembling the cabin, roof first, upside down, rafters in progress. Rafters? I could imagine building a cabin with two lengths of dowel; here he had a dozen, meticulously marked and cut and jointed. Two window frames, half-built, remained assembled. I couldn't picture how to puzzle the logs together without a blueprint, nor could seven-year-old Ted, though he had been expected to. I imagined the one sudden meaty swipe from Randy that sent their half-finished project flying, and saw the horror and shock on a little boy who just wanted to use a saw.

Ted's hands empty and sticky, he could find no home for them in his pockets or clasped together in front. He looked up at me, his face all innocence and shame. "It was my fault. I didn't know . . . which piece . . ."

Heartbreak.

Randy had been the faultless friend in college, a male Mary Poppins: practically perfect in every way. That he was contemptuous of hijinks and vice made him an easy foil for pranks, and his humorless pout at the time seemed more a gentle admonishment than scorn. But in close proximity and over the years, that reproach, of which he was always above, soured into outright intolerance and oppressive judgment.

And temper.

At first I had resisted more, always out of earshot of the children. But I wore down. And there was always some business stress that justified his mood, just as there was always some business task to bury myself in, with which to buy another day, and buy another week. This meal to be cooked, that office to be cleaned, those payroll checks to write. Things will get better.

———

At Mountain States Legal Foundation, Perry Pendley and Todd Welch tag-teamed to explain just what they were looking for in a case. I felt like a first-year law student who had forgotten to read the assignment beforehand.

"It's the equal protection clause," Perry said, "of the Fourteenth Amendment, and the due process clause of the Fifth for a federal matter. That's where the constitution says people need to be treated equally. This is the foundation for our suit, where we get the question: 'Does the equal protection guarantee forbid the federal government from awarding contracts on the basis of race?'"

"The problem is," said Todd, "that we can't just challenge some program that's in place. We have to show a specific injury from that program."

"It's not enough just that's it's unfair?" I asked. "That it's the government doing the discriminating?"

"That's not enough," he went on. "The way the law is created and changed is by happenstance as much as anything else. You have to find a perfect set of facts to get the issue before the court."

"So what would our perfect case look like?"

"It has to be a federal job—not state or private—so that when it's ruled unconstitutional the fix has to come at the federal level, not by striking down some state or local regulation."

Eighty percent of Adarand's work came from government contracts, almost all in Colorado. Of that, most was state work, but there were some national forest lands we had bid on recently, in the southwest corner of the state.

Todd continued. "Plus, there has to be a clear situation where a white contractor didn't get the job and a minority contractor did, even though the white contractor's bid was better. And we have to be able to prove that. This means gathering depositions, in person, from a cooperative prime contractor. And I'll need Randy with me, to help ask the right questions."

There were a few prime contractors in the state we might be able to count on to convey that message. But I could imagine the significant legwork and politicking it would take for Randy to help gather those statements, all while continuing to run a business. It would mean he would be home less.

Perry took over. "You need to know, Val, that federal lawyers do not want a decision the same way we do. Their job is to defend the laws in place, which means that their order of battle is to get cases thrown out however they can. I'm going a little inside baseball here on you, but there are three things you have to have when you file a lawsuit against the feds."

He held up his fist, and popped open the first finger.

"Number one, you got hurt. You, specifically got hurt in a unique way that's limited to you. In other words, you didn't just pay your taxes and the government spent your money foolishly like they did everybody else's money."

Every job lost to a higher bidder hurt us specifically; any of those would qualify. His second finger opened.

"Number two, you can trace your injury to the government official you just filed a suit against. It wasn't some intervening third party like a state government who did it; this is the guy you're suing."

The two lawyers had already explained that contract awards and the DBE designations traced directly to the Secretary of Transportation. That department is our target. Ring finger in the air.

"The third thing is that if you win, the judge can make you whole. It has what we call redressability. I'm not saying can he make all the pain go away, but can he deal with this injustice that you're facing? Can he strike down a program or set of regulations that are unconstitutional? For our purposes, the Supremes can; lower courts can't."

I just wanted the law changed, the program that classified people into boxes and put Michael Jordan and the Sultan of Brunei into the "disadvantaged" category—and made taxpayers pay their bonuses. I traced the provenance of a recent lost bid, for guardrail work in the San Juan National Forest. The U.S. Forest Service doesn't build its own roads in those national forests. In Colorado and ten other western states it contracts through the Central Federal Lands Highway Division, which is part of the Federal Highway Administration, which is part of the Department of Transportation. Every step federal.

I looked at them both, the firebrand who would become our speaker and the stalwart who would become our guide. I had our case.

"Gonzalez."

My great grandfather, Emil Linke, early 1900s

Losing Appeal

"This is the way it's going to unfold: Lose, Lose, Pray, Win."

ATTORNEY TODD WELCH

"We have to lose at District, lose at Circuit, appeal to the Supreme Court and pray they choose to take our case . . . and then convince five justices for the win," said our attorney Todd Welch, laying out the only strategy that could change the national precedents that had been allowing contract preferences to be doled out based on race. "Any earlier win, and we lose."

Mountain States Legal Foundation had just filed our initial complaint against the Department of Transportation, in Colorado's Federal District Court, for a case that would come to be called Adarand v Peña, naming the Secretary of Transportation.

"And this will take five years."

I considered what five more years with my co-plaintiff meant, that Randy and I would be facing the type of effort and business stress that had him crisscrossing the state all summer gathering depositions with Todd, while also bidding jobs, supervising work crews, and managing all the finances. "So, realistically," I asked, "what are our chances that even when we get through all those appeals—and lose—that our final appeal, the one to the Supreme Court, is one the Justices will even choose to hear?"

"One percent."

Each year, the United States Supreme Court hears about eighty of the eight thousand or so cases presented to them, almost all of which are appeals: no witnesses, no new evidence, just arguments. Although the exact reasons that our highest court chooses which cases to accept remain secreted within discussion chambers to which only nine are privy, certain patterns emerge, including the recognition that cases with greater national impact cross their threshold of consideration. Discriminating against an entire class of citizens just because their skin happens to be white should merit at least some scrutiny.

When my great-grandfather Emil Linke crossed the country to homestead the family ranch in Granby in 1883, he knew it would be five years of work before his 160 acres was sufficiently "proved up" for him to be granted clear title. For my father, raising champion Orr steers took generations of meticulous breeding and care. My family taught me to embrace the long game—for the right cause.

Another cause worth fighting at the time was as difficult and more personal than the broader one we were starting in the court system. The time had also arrived to address my mother's drinking head-on.

———

Cally Dally Many Dots leapt out of my lap when the phone rang. After two days with us she had not yet acclimated to the punctuated quiet of a private family home, or to gaining purchase on a newly waxed oak floor. Splays of adorable spots and paws gangled their way to momentary purchase underneath the kitchen table, one black-ringed eye visible from the shadows. I got to the receiver on the fourth ring.

"What took so long this time?" My mother's gin voice.

"Mom, it's two in the afternoon. How long have you been drinking?"

"It's just Tanqueray. You'll need it too, when your daughter stops talking to you."

Since bringing Ted and Kendra home after a summer on the ranch, Randy and I had settled them into a new school year, chased deponents across the state, begun viewing properties where we might build a bigger family home, and purchased the world's cutest Dalmatian puppy. Six weeks had passed quickly.

"Lemme talk to my grandkids. At least they still appreciate me."

"It's. *Two.* They're still in school." Third and fourth grade. I looked for Cally. She had backed out of sight.

"Maybe at school they'll learn some manners," she said. "Like gratitude."

"They spent most of the summer with you! What more do you want?"

"I want you to teach them how to say 'Thank you.' You sure never did."

Says the mother whose children raised themselves since before puberty. "Mom, I need to get them soon. I won't talk to you like this."

"And that's what's wrong with you, never making time. You're just ungrateful is what you are. We gave you everything."

You gave me heartache and mortification. You gave me a childhood without approval. But you also gave me escape from the Kremmling's tiny soda-straw worldview, by exposing me to dance and music and theater. You gave me pride in watching you excel in political circles, taking on any size fight. And you gave me an appreciation for conviction and hard work.

She wasn't done with her tirade. "By God, you don't know how good you had it! You and your brothers had silver spoons growing up. There were so many times we—"

I cradled the handset. Most of all, you gave me a loathing of talking to you when you've been drinking.

I wouldn't speak to my mother again for six months, not until well after the intervention date.

———

"We're on the docket: April 24 next year." Todd's call interrupted my work on the Adarand employee handbook. Randy ran the business, but was less reliable about legal niceties. Such details fell to me.

In the months since we filed our initial lawsuit, the Colorado Federal Court had assigned a judge, coordinated schedules with our team and the federal attorneys, and issued a case management order—the schedule whose last line reads, "trial date."

The date was so far in the future. "I guess I have plenty of time to get a new pair of boots and a Sunday-go-to-meetin' dress?"

"Not for this one," Todd said. "There won't be any oral arguments, because there just aren't any disputes *on fact* that call for courtroom resolution. Nobody disagrees about what happened."

"So, what does the April date even mean?" I had to ask.

Todd was by now accustomed to my inevitable questions. We had both learned that Randy's interest ended after following any instructions to sign here. "We file cross-motions for summary judgment," he said. "That means we and the feds both ask the District Court to dismiss the other side's case, straight up. We attach our brief arguing that this practice is unconstitutional discrimination based on race, and needs to stop. The feds say this is just the way the laws are written and that our case should be tossed."

I had to know if there was a flaw in the system. "You say we want to lose here. Does that mean you don't really try hard yet—you don't actually want to win?"

"Nice try," Todd said, "but we argue our hardest. All of this goes into the record for the appeals process, and we need to have our strongest case as part of the history at every step. We can hope that the people will start to see that our case makes sense, but to a certain extent, the judges at these lower court levels are powerless. The way the laws and precedent read, they really have no latitude. And we wouldn't want them to award us a win now anyway, at the local District level. A victory at Denver applies only here."

Our Mountain States attorneys made sure that Randy and I understood the hierarchy of our federal court system. In the United States there are ninety-four federal district courts, general trial courts with original jurisdictions where cases—a quarter million a year—are tried, juries serve, and witnesses testify. Colorado was one such federal district, and we had to lose there to get our case heard at the Tenth Circuit Court of Appeals. If the District Court of Colorado made a decision in our favor, then it created precedent only for our district, but our aims were higher than that, higher even than the six states comprising the Tenth Circuit.

The thirteen United States circuit courts are appellate courts, just like the Supreme Court. That meant no testimony or additional evidence in their venue, only arguments based on elements already in the record. Which meant that our case had to be rock-solid in the briefs that Mountain States would submit next April. Which meant hundreds of hours of research and depositions. Which made me even more grateful for their pro bono work on our behalf, and their commitment to rejecting the concept of racial or gender inferiority. Allies in fairness meant everything, especially when allies at home were hard to find.

———

"Your mother and I are going to get a divorce," my father said through tears. We had never seen him cry before, not when he almost lost the ranch in hard times, not when his own parents died, not when his children's accomplishments might have filled him with pride. "I moved some things down from the ranch. I'll be staying at the house in Golden."

My brothers Clair and Ed muttered acknowledgment. Ed said, "We all know something has to change. But isn't there another problem here, a bigger problem? Isn't it the bottle? Hasn't it always been?"

"She is a different person with that. Mean," Dad said. "I feel alone when I'm with her."

Clair leaned in. "You two are adults. You should be able to figure something out."

Jack picked up his Open Road Stetson, ran his fingers over the custom brim roll: bent up high on the sides so the cattle rope wouldn't catch. A brief dinner out with his children had already cost him more words than he was accustomed, especially as one hearing advice, not one giving orders. "I can't take it any more."

I considered my last conversation with my mother, how small and injured it had left me, and how resolved I had become to never again endure that verbal abuse. Since then I had aggressively researched alcoholism and its new treatments, spurred by the recently publicized struggles of local billionaire Bill Daniels, and inspired by his writings on the value of treatment at a time when alcoholism was seldom admitted, even privately. Cable TV pioneer Bill Daniels, a recovered alcoholic who fifteen years prior had run for Governor of Colorado, and for whose candidacy Valery Orr had stuffed envelopes and Alta Orr had campaigned door to door. And who counted Alta Orr among his treasured friends.

"There might be another option."

———

"We have a problem."

I heard Todd Welch's voice through the handset. Randy handed me the phone. "It's for you." Problems were always for me.

"Todd, what's going on?"

"We learned today that District Court denied our motion for summary judgment."

Randy overheard. He was crestfallen. He had never seemed to internalize the need for us to fail at first so that we could escalate the case to the proper venue. The dismissal was necessary, but it was still a loss. Randy didn't lose anything with grace.

"We needed that to happen, right?' I asked Todd. "This is good news. Now we can appeal." It was already well over a year since our filing of cross-motions for summary judgment, and almost two years since our initial complaint. It was time to get our case in front of the Tenth.

Randy walked back to his office to complete yet one more set of financial statements to support our mortgage application. Our offer to buy two and one-half acres in Monument had only recently been accepted, and we were both anxious to design and build the sanctuary in which to raise two children through high school. The bank was voracious demanding documentation and financials. Randy was unpleasant collating and delivering them.

Todd said, "Valery, they denied our motion three months ago, on April 21. We were never notified." Today was July 17.

I tried not to sigh out loud. Losing those three months might not matter to Mountain States Legal, but until this law was changed, Randy's continued grumbling about being passed over for jobs wasn't going to stop. I put on a brave voice. "So we lost three months on our calendar. I guess that's going to have to be OK."

"I'm trying to tell you," he said. "There's a time limit for our appeal to the Tenth Circuit."

"How many months is the limit?"

"Thirty days."

———

Interventionist John LaSalle said, "I know how hard this is, and how much you all love Alta."

It was the day before. At nearby Centennial airport Bill Daniels' private Learjet stood fueled, its flight plan filed, the pilot on stand-by.

"You're giving her a gift—one nobody else can give her—but it comes with a price. The gift is wrapped in the cloth of shock: she cannot know in advance of the intervention. She cannot. Without a sudden and dramatic jolt, the process fails. We've seen it happen enough to know that we can't proceed without it. Only together and as a surprise can we convey the value of what's needed. We have to be united and strong in this."

Murmured yeses and tearful nods from everyone: Ed and Susie, hands clasped; Fred and Vicki, somber and small; Clair and Deb, their drawn and distant expressions revealing the demands of their own struggles; Jack, lost in middle age, a cattleman unhorsed; and me without Randy, whose presence would only add judgment and remove compassion.

Clair prayed. We all joined hands.

"Amen."

Jack let go first.

In twelve hours my mother would be aloft, accompanied by John LaSalle to the Betty Ford Clinic in Rancho Mirage, California, there to find the person we had all been missing for decades. Months of research and countless interviews with treatment centers had convinced me that this option was my mother's best hope. Bill Daniels had meant it when he told me he would do anything he could to help. My brothers and father had consented, enthusiastically, and now we had finally finished all of the preparation, all for one surprise meeting at the ranch tomorrow, followed by the best alcoholism treatment available at any price.

I drove home. My brothers and their wives drove home. Jack drove to tell Alta.

———

The Tenth Circuit Court of Appeals, at what was the Denver United States Post Office and Courthouse, and what would be renamed four months later the Byron White United States Courthouse, is fronted by sixteen massive Ionic columns, supporting the building's stately neo-classical grandeur. The broad arched halls and courtrooms within are equally majestic. We waited outside the courtroom, ready for oral arguments, my reluctant co-plaintiff and my team of lawyers, all full of decorum and hushed tones.

Mountain States Legal Foundation had been preparing the case for three years, and for the last week lead attorney Perry Pendley had been reviewing, practicing, and refining his arguments for this District Court appeal. As written, the law was against us, but inside the courtroom a strong team took no chances, and was prepared to capitalize on any mistakes.

Click-click-click-click-click-click.

We turned to see a petite and smartly dressed woman running through the halls in high heels. *Click-click-click-click-click-click.*

"Is this where Adarand's being argued?" she asked, breathless.

I was impressed that someone was interested enough in our case to rush through a federal courthouse in order to not miss any of the proceedings. There would be plenty of room in the gallery to watch. Nobody else was here besides us. We had not even spotted opposing counsel yet.

"Don't worry, it hasn't started," said Perry, towering over her and her heels. "I'm arguing it."

"Good." She smoothed out her skirt. Took three deep breaths. "I'm from the Justice Department. I'm arguing the other side."

Perry tipped his head to one side, clearly nonplussed. "Aren't you cutting it kind of close?"

"Well, I just found out yesterday that I'd be here. The person who was supposed to argue it got sick and they said, 'Would you go out and argue Adarand?' So I hopped on a plane."

"Oh." Perry's famous eloquence escaped him momentarily. "Sure."

That's how slam-dunk the Justice Department viewed our case, how much the law as written was unequivocally against us. How much we had no chance on this appeal of the Denver District Court's decision.

The same confidence had suffused the Justice Department's attitude when, a year prior, we had been forced to reach out to them after having missed by two months the deadline to file the appeal. They hadn't been notified either, and both because it was the ethical thing to do and because they didn't want to lose the case on a technicality, only to have a similar one come close behind, had agreed to allow the tardy appeal.

They knew it wouldn't matter in any case.

Of course we lost.

———

A few things about Jack Orr were starting to make sense. Things like why he avoided higher office, despite my mother's entrenchment for years in the Colorado political machinery. Despite her running for University of Colorado Regent. Despite her being state vice-chair of the Colorado Republican Party. Despite his lobbying Governors on behalf of the Colorado Cattlemen and contributing thousands to Republican candidates. And despite being asked to serve as Ronald Reagan's Secretary of Agriculture.

In the late 70s Jack Orr's eminence as a cattleman and conviction as a conservative fostered acquaintances of influence. He showed ranches to Steve Forbes, traded livestock tips with John Wayne, and discussed agricultural policies with Ronald Reagan. And yet when Reagan asked him to serve on his cabinet, my father demurred.

Alta was the reason. She was his excuse.

"You can find somebody else," he would say, when asked to run for Governor in the 1970s.

"I just need to work," he told the new president back in 1981.

"I won't tell Alta about the intervention," he told his children a decade later.

My father was as addicted to the fight with her as she was to the bottle. That fight and her flaw was a battlefield he knew, one that, in spite of his denials, he refused to abandon. He was attached to her addiction and the unspoken excuse it gave him to avoid the brightest spotlight. Jack protected my mother's reputation by remaining away from the scrutiny a higher public office would bring. Alta protected him by allowing him to remain on familiar ground, on ranches he had known since childhood—since driving cattle at the age of four.

And none of that could be altered by words from me or my brothers, so we stopped trying. For my part, I erected boundaries on behalf of my children and me: no contact when Mom is drinking.

You can't always train a bull to stand still for the show ring. Sometimes, you just need to build a stronger fence.

———

The United States Court of Appeals for the Tenth Circuit has appellate jurisdiction over six states: Colorado, Kansas, New Mexico, Wyoming, Utah, and Oklahoma. As part of our "Lose, Lose, Pray, Win" strategy, it demarked our second loss. But they had to hear our case: the Tenth has mandatory appeal, which means that it must hear every one of the five thousand or so cases presented every year. The district- and circuit-level components of our plan were procedure and clockwork. Not so with the Supreme Court. For them we had to pray.

But first we had to write a *petition for writ of certiorari*, a specific pleading that asks the court to hear our case. If the Supreme Court finds our circumstances compelling enough, they will approve the petition—they will grant *cert*.

At Mountain States Legal Foundation, since our Tenth Circuit loss, the team had spent months crafting the application for cert. At home, reading from the judge's ruling in the case the Tenth Court upheld, I was explaining the nuance to First Degree Air Force Cadet Joe Nance.

"Stick with me. Here's what we're up against."

"I'm listening," he said, and he meant it. Joe always listened.

Four years ago our family met Joe as part of the Air Force Academy's Sponsor Families Program, like adopting a foreign exchange student, but without the language barrier. My father used his ranch to give errant boys opportunities that their circumstances had not allowed; I wanted to use our family to give servicemen some respite from the

Academy regimen—a home away from home for young airmen in training. When the Academy granted occasional leave, we had a house-guest, my children had a role model, and I had one man in the house who would discuss the case. When he wasn't catching up on sleep.

"Two years ago—April '92—the Denver District Court judge ruled that the law was against us. That's the law we challenged in 1990 when we initially filed suit and the ruling the Circuit Court just upheld." After four years under Mountain States' tutelage I had grasped the legal background well enough, but explaining it out loud helped. "We understand that race preferences are unfair, but even if District Judge Carrigan agreed with us, he couldn't apply any judgment in the matter. The law was clear."

I handed Joe a beer. He was almost twenty-one, and graduating this summer. Old enough to serve the country is old enough to drink.

"Unfortunate as it is, the government can legally discriminate," I said. "But there are limits, and Judge Carrigan said so." I read from his April 21, 1992 ruling:

"Thus *Fullilove*, *Croson* and *Metro Broadcasting* teach that the federal government can, by virtue of the enforcement clause of the Fourteenth Amendment, engage in affirmative action with a freer hand than states and municipalities."

After four years at a military academy, Joe had practice at identifying the crux of a matter. If he were in class, he would be taking notes. In lieu, he took a sip.

I pointed at Carrigan's text. "Those precedents the judge mentions—that's our case law. Croson is good law. Fullilove and Metro are bad."

"You know I'm studying engineering, right?" he said. "Not law."

"Almost done. Turns out the two most rigorous standards the government can use to justify its reverse discrimination are intermediate scrutiny and strict scrutiny. Both are bad, but intermediate scrutiny is worse. It says they only have to be 'remedying discrimination.' It's a loose standard that applies to national laws and contracts."

"Got it," he said. "The feds can set up these race-based set-asides as a general remedy for whatever program they want, as long as they say it's fixing past discrimination."

"And states can't," I said. "That's why Croson is good. It says that states have to apply strict scrutiny to justify race preferences. That means their action has to be remedying a specific discrimination of an individual—not just a general history of discrimination against a group—and that's a much higher standard."

"So you want the federal laws, like the contracts Adarand bids on, to have to use this strict scrutiny standard like in Croson? That will eliminate the set-asides?"

"What we want is to remove government-sponsored discrimination entirely. But we'll take tighter restrictions and call it progress."

Joe tapped his empty bottle. "What I want is extra credit for this after-hours study. The judge mentioned other cases. Metro and Fullilove?"

"Save it for another day. There's not enough beer in the house for that."

———

"My workload just tripled," said Todd Welch.

I appreciated hearing his voice on my phone, even when there was no visible progress on the case. Todd's demeanor always reflected a quiet assurance that our journey had direction and purpose, as if he had been granted a divine preview of events to come.

"They granted cert," he said. "The United States Supreme Court just agreed to hear your case. We're taking Adarand to Washington."

Stunned motionless in my new bedroom, I caught my breath. I kept the cordless to my ear but couldn't form any words. In the slant of my carved cheval mirror I saw myself hearing the news I had been awaiting for five years: mouth agape, one person still and small. This is what humility looks like.

"Some time in January," he said. It was now late September. "The clerk there just called me. The clerk of the Supreme Court."

Todd's animated voice betrayed any pretense of equanimity. This mattered, every part of it, even to experienced litigators.

"I've told Perry and the Mountain States team, and you won't be surprised to hear that they are all euphoric. Cloud nine. Especially since we had never done this before, never written a petition for cert."

"Now you tell me! I thought you were old hands at this."

"Just beginners' luck for a couple of Wyoming country boys."

I walked from the bedroom across new marble and Berber, past glass banisters and antique tables into a prismatic spray of mid-afternoon rainbows, teased color-by-color from the Colorado sun through my favorite crystal chandelier. This tiny construction company in Colorado Springs, this ranch girl, this American, would be heard by the highest court in the land. I felt the white and heat of the sun, and sought the facets of red and blue. There were many. I loved my country.

"Todd, we're about to be a part of history."

"We are. And Val. Thank you." He clicked off.

Thank *me*? All I did was persevere. You did the work. You kept on when others would have stopped. When Randy would have stopped.

I called him at the Adarand office. He had not heard. He took the news. Gave nothing back. Got back to work.

Fuck him and his detached indifference.

I had all the allies I needed. I had Perry and Todd and the Mountain States team. I had cadet Joe for grounding and brothers for cheerleading. I had middle-school children who for the next four months would be living a civics lesson that I would make sure they understood. And I had years in my own saddle, riding fence and corralling steers.

I looked up at what is still my favorite piece of art, an original from Carrie Fell called "Outdistancing the Blue." Her vibrant acrylic and oil show two horsemen in abstract, indigo and crimson, heads down in full gallop. Damn right.

Five years earlier I sat across an after-dinner table, fed up with hearing Randy complain about losing another job for being white. Stop complaining and do something, I told him.

Oh, we're doing something.

Ted, age fifteen, and Kendra, age fourteen, on the steps of the United States Supreme Court

The Highest Court

"Equal Justice Under Law"

INCISED ON THE ARCHITRAVE OF THE U.S. SUPREME COURT BUILDING

January came quickly.

After years of lower-court preparation, making arguments that we knew would be rejected, we now had the opportunity to change the laws themselves, the ones that reduced people to checkboxes: black, brown, red, yellow, white. I hated those boxes.

At home we each had our roles. Kendra and Ted readied for the civil rights lesson we were undertaking. I was legal liaison, logistics officer, and cheerleader. Randy ran Adarand and became the face of the case.

"We need one person to put in front of the public, to be the spokesperson." I said to Randy.

"Yup."

"Someone who not only knows the business well, but can also talk about the unfairness firsthand."

"Sure."

"People don't relate well to lawyers, so it needs to be someone in Adarand, don't you think?"

"Fine."

"I'm the biggest shareholder, but I can't speak to the operations, and Steve—well, we just can't put him in front of the camera."

"OK."

"Which leaves you. Are you up for that?"

"Whatever. But I really don't like this, and I will never, ever give a speech."

"Whatever."

And so Randy Pech became our media front, representing the cause on radio, print, and television, the face of White America: a businessman who started with practically nothing and built a quality company from scratch. He looked the part, a normal Joe, wife and two kids, working for the American Dream. Soft-spoken, average looking, a regular guy who just wanted a fair shake.

And yet the press dubbed him the "Angry White Male." Of course they had it wrong. On screen and on the page Randy was never angry. Never in public.

I rallied the troops. In a simple plaque I found our guide star. It read: "Do not do what others consider to be great, but what you consider to be right." Hanging it at eye level in our Adarand office, I told Randy, "We must never lose sight of this because, if we do, then it's not worth doing." He allowed the sign to stay. I had "Equal Justice Under Law" engraved on square marble paperweights—one for each member of our legal team. I had my children prepare journals for the trip, items later recognized for school credit. I arranged for my parents to meet us in Washington.

But before reaching the nation's capital, we started in New York City. Excerpts from my children's journals tell it best.

TED'S JOURNAL: JANUARY 6, 1995

. . . Seeing the lights of New York as we flew in. The lights of the city were spectacular to look at . . .

KENDRA'S JOURNAL: JANUARY 6, 1995

. . . When we came in to New York the city seemed to go on forever, it as if it were all sparkling gold . . .

TED'S JOURNAL: JANUARY 7, 1995

. . . went to a show named, "STOMP" at the Orpheum theatre and it was really really really one of the best shows I've ever seen . . .

KENDRA'S JOURNAL: JANUARY 7, 1995

. . . I couldn't dry my hair because my dad was in an interview with the Washington Post . . .

TED'S JOURNAL: JANUARY 8, 1995

. . . we caught a ferry to Ellis Island where immigrants like my ancestors became U.S. citizens. After that little tour we walked to the World Trade Center and went all the way to the top of the tower . . .

Randy refused the elevator ride. It was too high. Seven years later his opportunity was lost forever.

KENDRA'S JOURNAL: JANUARY 8, 1995

. . . My favorite was the Statue of Liberty. It's humungous and green. I loved it. It's really pretty. Ellis Island was an island where immigrants came to from different countries to get signed up here. They would check you for any diseases and ask what you would do for this country . . .

> TED'S JOURNAL: JANUARY 9, 1995
>
> . . . we walked to Central Park and took a carriage around the park. Kendra and I went to FAO Schwarz . . .

> KENDRA'S JOURNAL: JANUARY 9, 1995
>
> . . . asked a couple people where the best restaurants were. They suggested Bill Hong's. The best dinner so far. Michael Jackson goes there a lot to eat and other famous people. That's how good it is . . .

> TED'S JOURNAL: JANUARY 10, 1995
>
> . . . This is the first train I've ever been on in my whole long life. The various stops were New Jersey, Philadelphia, and some other cities. Oh! One more thing, the former wife of Martin Luther King stayed in this room before us, the night before . . .

> KENDRA'S JOURNAL: JANUARY 10, 1995
>
> . . . This motel is the Lowes L'Enfant Plaza. The bell hop told us that the King family stayed in our suite the night before . . .

In my view we were fighting for the same exact thing that Coretta Scott King's husband fought for—simple equality.

> KENDRA'S JOURNAL: JANUARY 11, 1995
>
> . . . My dad had two interviews today and got a million pictures taken of him. Came to the motel to meet my "adopted" brother Joe who graduated from U.S. Air Force Academy and is now stationed in Boston and Washington. Decided to walk to the White House— beautiful with lots of fountains . . .

> TED'S JOURNAL: JANUARY 11, 1995
>
> *... we walked to the Capitol building where the House of Represen-*
> *tatives and Senate meet. The Great Rotunda is the central ceremo-*
> *nial space of the Capitol. When JFK died he was placed in there for*
> *a few days so people could give there last respects ...*

I spent a little extra time in the rotunda, remembering November 22, 1963.

> TED'S JOURNAL: JANUARY 12, 1995
>
> *... We started the day by getting ready for my dad's interview with*
> *CNN. Then we rode the Metro to the Washington Monument. As*
> *soon as we got down we walked to the Lincoln Memorial ...*

> KENDRA'S JOURNAL: JANUARY 12, 1995
>
> *... Walked across a park to reflecting pond and down to the Lin-*
> *coln Memorial where Martin Luther King made his "I have a*
> *dream" speech ...*

> TED'S JOURNAL: JANUARY 13, 1995
>
> *... Today we went to the Pentagon to meet our cadet Joe Nance.*
> *The Pentagon is big enough to hold 5 Capitol buildings and is 2½*
> *miles long if you walk around it ...*

> KENDRA'S JOURNAL: JANUARY 13, 1995
>
> *... meet our Cadet, Joe—well actually he's not a cadet anymore*
> *he is a Second Lt. and works at the Pentagon. Next stop was the*
> *United States Holocaust Memorial Museum. If you had blond hair*
> *and blue eyes you were considered superior but dark hair and*
> *dark eyes were considered bad ...*

> TED'S JOURNAL: JANUARY 14, 1995
>
> *. . . This morning we met up with my grandparents and our cadet Joe Nance in a 2½ hour drive to Gettysburg. The brochure says that if you find some bones lying around near a battlefield it might just be a soldiers bones . . .*

> KENDRA'S JOURNAL: JANUARY 14, 1995
>
> *. . . Today our plan was to go to Gettysburg. More people died in the three day war then did in the Vietnam War . . .*

> KENDRA'S JOURNAL: JANUARY 15, 1995
>
> *. . . headed to Annapolis to visit the Naval Academy. . .*

Joe and his fellow ex-cadet Jeremy took the kids to Annapolis, since we had interviews all day. Our family had welcomed Jeremy as an add-on adoptee during his and Joe's last year at the Air Force Academy.

The rest of us had a day of cameras and microphones. It seemed that Randy always got more time in front of a mic than he wanted, and Perry always got less than he deserved.

> TED'S JOURNAL: JANUARY 15, 1995
>
> *. . . After all of us got back, went swimming for almost 2½ hours. We got back to the hotel and talked for maybe 30 minutes . . .*

> KENDRA'S JOURNAL: JANUARY 16, 1995
>
> *. . . My grandpa, grandma, Mom, and me all went to Mt. Vernon . . .*

Randy refused to go. He was too stressed. Ted babysat him.

TED'S JOURNAL: JANUARY 16, 1995

... my dad and I stayed back at the hotel while my sister, mom and grandparents went to Mt. Vernon ...

TED'S JOURNAL: JANUARY 17, 1995

... We met with Joe & Jeremy along with our grandparents to stand in line at the Supreme Court building. We had reserved seats but Joe, Jeremy and our grandparents did not ...

A broad oval plaza fronts the Supreme Court building, with circular fountains on each side and statues representing justice and law guarding the expanse. Steps up and east take one through its massive bronze doors; steps down and west lead directly across First Street NE to the Capitol. We stamped for warmth on the plaza's marble underfoot.

Although the Supreme Court building and its proceedings are open to the public, its capacity is limited, and lines form early for contentious cases. We arrived two hours before sunrise to find perhaps twenty already in line, few enough to ensure that everyone in our group would get in.

On this dark, cold, winter morning, our entire family stood together, even those of us with reserved seats. The lawyers came later. The airmen volunteered to find cocoa, and I walked to the head of the line, curious to see what brought others here so early.

I asked incognito and innocently, "Are you here for the Adarand case?" Partisanship seemed to parallel race. Blacks feared losing their race preferences (affirmative action, they were always sure to call it). Younger whites and assorted other minorities sympathized. Older whites hoped to see the government get out of the race business. But everyone had a stake in the outcome—everyone but one.

"Pat O'Rourke, Ma'am."

So polite. "And you're a law student?"

"Georgetown. It's a beautiful area, just across the river from Arlington."

"What brings you here for this case?" I asked.

He unshouldered his pack and set it on the ground. "It's our final assignment for a seminar class. We each had to pick a case for this term, and this one caught my eye. It's an important topic. It looks close; could go either way. I'll have to write an opinion, and it's more interesting to explore issues where the court's in flux, like affirmative action."

"So how do you think they'll rule?"

"No way to know, of course. The Court does a remarkable job of keeping its work quiet. But I have to think it swings on O'Connor. And if it does, then it suggests an incremental decision. She's not the type to favor broad, sweeping opinions."

I wanted the broadest, most sweeping opinion possible. Perhaps something like, "The government cannot use race for anything, ever. It cannot ask your race. It cannot consider your race." Until a ruling like that, creating a meritocracy instead of a minoritocracy, we would continue to inflame race differences and move farther apart as a country.

"Oh, and one more thing that made this case interesting for me," Pat said. "The plaintiffs are from my home town."

"The plaintiffs?" I realized that I had not yet introduced myself.

"Yeah," he said. "Colorado Springs."

Over the next four hours I watched the line grow, down the steps and across the patio. Many in it would be relegated to the three-minute line, gaining only a brief pass through the proceedings; most would be turned away altogether.

Joe's return with hot chocolate restored some of the heat I had lost through my tapestry-print shoes.

"Look at the crowd, Joe. Look at their color." I disliked making a point of it, but the laws we were fighting demanded we consider skin color.

Joe Nance examined the growing line of hopefuls, each vying for a seat in the Highest Court in the Land. "Seems mixed? We could be any place in the country."

"Anyplace." I wrapped both hands around the cup. "So which of these people deserve preferences based on race? Maybe the protestors across the street—the ones with signs? They're all black."

"Maybe not anybody?"

"Well sure, now, but back in the 60s I'll say African Americans. They were only ten percent of the population then, and suffering tremendous, real discrimination." I inhaled deeply of the sweet steam.

Joe played along. He had been my legal sounding board for years, and knew the drill. Besides, anything to distract us from the cold. "That was then. That's why we had the Civil Rights Act."

"Necessary then, but now it's grown all out of proportion. Now it's this giant blanket of presumption. The government *presumes* that you're disadvantaged just because you're in some group." I pointed at the main court entrance, at the massive lintel resting on its sixteen marble columns, at the incision thereon: "Equal Justice Under Law."

"What's equal about it when the list of disadvantaged groups is now sixty-five percent of the population?" I said, between sips. "If so many people claim disadvantage—blacks, Hispanics, women, veterans, Pacific Islanders, recent immigrants, native Americans, and ridiculous amounts more—isn't it about time to simplify it all and let us compete on our merits?"

"Maybe you should be arguing the case."

"Wait until you hear Perry." He and Todd Welch had recently completed several mock trial exercises, where Perry honed his arguments against a barrage of questions from heavy-hitting jurists, among them John Roberts, current Chief Justice of the Supreme Court, but at the time representing the Associated General Contractors with an amicus—friend of the court—brief. But no amount of practice could equate to the Supreme Court, the ultimate "hot court," one in which the justices are fully intimate with the case beforehand, and ready to demonstrate that preparation with active and arcane questions directed not so much to the appellant as to the other justices. A hot court does not wait passively for plaintiff's argument to conclude.

Nonetheless, although Perry was the proper man to argue the case, Todd was the behind-the-scenes workhorse. He took all the depositions, did the research, and wrote the briefs. That homework, combined with Perry's meticulous study, resulted in a team ready for any venue.

In addition to being exactingly prepared, Perry was also properly dressed for the job. In every court appearance to date Perry wore his bespoke blue button-down-collar shirts. Very natty. But yesterday John Roberts had taken him aside.

"Perry, you do have a white shirt, don't you?"

"No, I've got a suitcase full of blue shirts."

"You're going to need a white shirt," said the man who would go on to prevail in twenty-five Supreme Court arguments before his appointment to the highest court. "And they can't be button-down. The Chief is crazy about button-down shirts."

Any advice, even fashion tips, from John Roberts carried weight, which explained why Perry wore a new crisp white shirt that morning, one he purchased and had cleaned the night before, its unnoticed dry-cleaning tag still attached.

At 9:30 the 6½-ton bronze doors slid aside, rolling into pockets in the wall. I expected the elegance and quiet of the Great Hall beyond, with its pink marble columns and busts of past chief justices, and from church I thought I knew reverence, but the dignity of God's House, I decided as a young girl, was within. This hall carried its consecration without. This hall had a surpassing importance and dignity, an immensity and depth that spoke truth. I did not expect the awe that grew with every step.

United States Supreme Court chambers

Nor did I expect the weight, the palpable heaviness. I felt the gravity of our We-the-People communal bond, protected by the swords of authority and justice. I felt the heft of the Constitution, and of the country it created.

I felt history.

So much marble and velvet for such a little company.

And so tiny a courtroom for such an important institution.

The courtroom itself is smaller than any of the appellate courts where we argued, and the Bench is much closer. As appellants, we sat three rows behind the bronze railing that separated the public section from the Supreme Court Bar. Beyond the rail, in the Bar proper, were four tables, where attorneys for both morning cases already waited.

Perry took deep, measured breaths and deliberately closed his eyes for brief intervals. Settling his nerves. His brow glistened.

Between the tables, directly opposite the Chief Justice's seat, the lectern stood immediately facing the Bench, with no more than ten feet between. Intimately close.

Important work gets done here.

Before an attorney can argue before or submit documents to the Supreme Court, he or she must be a member of the Supreme Court Bar, as Perry Pendley already was. Most people file such paperwork remotely, via affidavit and mail, but those with the opportunity can ask for the swearing in person. Todd Welch and the remainder of the

Mountain States team rose and placed their right hands in the air. My friend's hand trembled.

As they all repeated after the Clerk, I listened to one. "I, Todd Welch, do solemnly swear that as an attorney and as a counselor of this Court, I will conduct myself uprightly and according to law, and that I will support the Constitution of the United States."

The Constitution of the United States. Of my United States. I was trembling.

They wheeled Brennan in. Liberal icon William Brennan retired from the Supreme Court in 1990, and died two years after this case. At eighty-eight, his confinement to a wheelchair reflected his declining health. Attendants settled his chair to the left of the Bench, near the Clerk.

Brennan's final majority opinion, issued on the last day of his Supreme Court tenure, was for Metro Broadcasting, the Court's most recent affirmative-action case. That ruling upheld granting blacks increased ownership in radio and television stations, based solely on their race. Issued so recently, Metro represented a stark barrier to Adarand for the principal of *stare decisis*, the idea that courts should abide by prior rulings and not disturb settled matters. A win for Adarand almost certainly meant overruling Metro.

A power play for moral suasion, or a show of respect to an ailing Justice?

In 1990, Brennan could cobble together five votes for race preferences, but the Court had changed.

> KENDRA'S JOURNAL: JANUARY 17, 1995
> *. . . They rang a bell and then slammed the gavel so we would rise for the Justices to enter . . .*

After a brief flurry of pomp and oyesses, Perry approached the lectern. "Mr. Chief Justice, and may it please the Court: Adarand is a small, family-owned corporation that does business in Colorado Springs, Colorado. It is owned by and operated by Randy Pech, his wife Valery—"

In their mock trial, John Roberts had told Perry that he had to personalize the case. "You're going to have a minute at most to tell the court who your client is," John said. "They know what the legal issues are; they know the cases. They need to know who your client is. You've got to put a face on your case. Tell a story."

Our story.

Soon the questions came rapid-fire. "Do we know that was the reason for the rejection?" "Does that clarify that it was the presumption that was crucial?" "The 8(a) certification, does that enter into this case?" "Do you contend that Congress failed to make adequate findings?"

To my left, the Angry White Male tried to pay attention, but he had never shown interest in the legal nuance, and today's constitutional chess match pivoted on the most arcane minutiae.

Perry had it all committed to memory, every citation and implication, with never a glance down at his notes. "We're challenging section 502 of the Small Business Act, which is section 644(g), which is contained at page 11-A of the Government's brief," he said, responding to Justice Ginsburg. "In addition, there is section 637(d), which is on page 11 of the Government's appendix, which sets out the presumption, and that presumption is applied to 644(g) because of the—"

To my right, Kendra leaned forward, elbows on knees, the warmth and the heady jargon weighing on her. Momentarily and discreetly an attendant corrected her. Whether for security or respect, all participants were obliged to sit up straight.

Everyone except the Chief Justice. From his center seat at the Bench, Justice Rehnquist rose, laced his fingers behind his back, and paced. The crowd suppressed a murmur, not recognizing his actions as merely a means to relieve his chronic back pain. Perry, warned beforehand, continued unimpeded.

Justice Souter: "Did your complaint specify the presumption as being the floah in the statutory scheme?" To a western girl, Justice Souter's New England inflection was hard to follow. Did he just say "floor," or something else?

For the first time, Perry hesitated. He appeared to be calculating. Four uncomfortable seconds passed before he finally gave up. "The . . . excuse me, Your Honor, the floor as to the—"

Justice Souter: "No, I . . . flaw."

Mr. Pendley: "Oh, flaw."

Justice Souter: "It's my regional accent."

Laughter in the Supreme Court is a rare treat. Even notoriously silent Justice Thomas cracked a smile. Perry regained his tempo and composure without hesitation. "It's my hearing."

The courtroom tension broke with that exchange, and Perry volleyed back the following intricate questions with increasing aplomb. When his white, five-minute light came on, he found the next opportunity to introduce the plain-language argument that even the recipients of set-asides didn't need them.

"The DBE's testified, 'We don't need the help. That's all very nice to have, but we're fine. We're perfectly capable of doing this job. We don't need that assistance.'" The Justices granted him a rare silence to complete his assertion. "On its face that's an impermissible racial stereotype to say all these DBE's out there are so incompetent that they need the help, when the fact is they don't."

And what does it say to them to get it anyway? What must it do to their esteem to not know whether they are being judged on their talents or on their pigments?

Our argument hinged on whether a business should be assumed to be disadvantaged just because its owner happened to be in one of twenty-six identified groups. By that logic, a Hong Kong banker or the son of landed gentry from Spain could buy a local construction company and claim disadvantage just to get the minority set-asides. As the

laws were written, it would be up to companies like ours to individu-
ally challenge those companies' claims of disadvantage. Besides the
reputation it would give us as being litigious troublemakers, the effort
and cost would be unreasonable to put on individual businesses. We
did not want to become factories for suing other companies—and get
blackballed because of it; we just wanted to put up fence.

When the Solicitor General, an African American appointed by
Bill Clinton, took the lectern to argue the government's case, Justice
Scalia revealed his bias towards our side.

Justice Scalia: "Do you have any example where somebody in the
position of Adarand successfully brought a challenge? Do you know of
any?"

Mr. Days, III: "It's very hard, Justice Scalia, to identify that, because—"

Justice Scalia: "You don't know of any."

Mr. Days, III: "That's correct."

The cliché is that you can't win a case with oral argument, but you
can lose one. I hoped the cliché had some truth for the opposing counsel.

But Scalia was only one of nine.

And then with a small red light on the lectern it was over. For
months the justices had already considered the case privately, but
thirty minutes per side publicly still seemed so tiny a conclusion for six
years of build-up. In a bustle and daze we recovered our checked coats
and bags, shuffled past clusters of brown-eyed glares, and stepped
back into sunlight and the bracing cold, to microphones everywhere.

And to a tag on Perry's sleeve. I caught his eye and tried to be subtle. With deft fingers he pulled it off, murmuring, "Oh my god, I was
just up there with that." How intent must the fastidious Perry have
been to overlook that? Proof he was fully on his legal game, if not his
sartorial one.

Todd pulled me aside. "I was shocked at how close the Justices
were. You cannot prepare yourself emotionally for being that close to
nine of the most powerful men and women in this country."

"Todd, I felt it too. Thank you. It was so worth it to stick through this. But let's never do that again."

We split up. I talked to CNBC; under my parents' watch, newspaper reporters questioned Ted and Kendra. On the broader plaza, in front of a knot of microphones, a crowd gathered for Randy and Perry. I soon broke free to hear an answer in progress.

"Because it's odious to a free society," Perry said. "Because it stigmatizes everybody. It stigmatizes the alleged beneficiaries by letting people think they are incompetent, that they can't handle programs without that assistance."

Amen. Perry said it fancier than I did, but with no more conviction. Race preferences degrade the people who get them.

Another buzz of questions, then Perry again. "It would be comparable if a city, instead of zoning an area whites-only, simply said we're going to pay every homeowner a bonus if they sell to a white person instead of a minority. That would be outrageous. We'd all be offended by it. And that's what the government is doing in this case. The government is paying people to make decisions based on race."

And just maybe, if Perry's argument last hour was strong enough, the nine justices inside might bring some of that to a halt.

> TED'S JOURNAL: JANUARY 17, 1995
>
> . . . From my mom and dad's case I learned that discrimination of any kind is wrong and that affirmative action will not help what happened or get rid of the past, all it will do is just make different races hate each other more and more.

> KENDRA'S JOURNAL: JANUARY 17, 1995
>
> . . . I'm so proud of my mom and dad for standing up for what they believe in.

Lincoln Leadership Awards, Mayflower Hotel, Washington DC: (L to R) Ted, Newt Gingrich, Perry Pendley, Val, Kendra

Equally Stifled

"Without affirmative action my opportunities may not be the same as my Caucasian peers."

NICOLE RETLAND, 7TH-GRADE HONOR STUDENT. BLACK.

"These programs stamp minorities with a badge of inferiority."

CLARENCE THOMAS, SUPREME COURT JUSTICE. BLACK.

All three major television networks led with the same story on June 12, 1995. Dan Rather at CBS: "The Court set new restrictions on federal affirmative action programs." Tom Brokaw at NBC: "Those standards make it much more difficult for affirmative action." Peter Jennings at ABC: "The power of the federal government to encourage the hiring of minorities will be quite severely limited."

We won.

Sort of.

In a nuanced, complex opinion, the Court determined that federal programs needed to conform to the same "strict scrutiny" standards that already applied to state and local programs. This is the most exacting level of judicial review, and means that any law must meet a "compelling government interest" and must be "narrowly tailored" to accomplish its goal.

I wanted the Court to abolish preferences altogether, but Justice Sandra Day O'Connor, writing the opinion for the 5-4 majority, made clear that she was not ready to go that far: "The unhappy persistence of both the practice and the lingering effects of racial discrimination against minorities in this country is an unfortunate reality and government is not disqualified from acting in response to it."

As a majority—and thus as law—the Court left in place its race-conscious programs, but tightened the standards. For our case, this meant that it was remanded back to the Tenth Circuit to determine whether the federal program under which we lost the San Juan National Forest contract could survive this new, tougher standard.

Although all we wanted to do was go back to work, we were instead going back to court.

I wished that five Justices had the backbone of Justices Clarence Thomas and Antonin Scalia. Their concurring opinions reflected a clear sense of how wrong these programs were. From Justice Thomas: "Under our Constitution, the government may not make distinctions on the basis of race. These programs stamp minorities with a badge of inferiority. . . In my mind, government-sponsored racial discrimination based on benign prejudice is just as noxious as discrimination inspired by malicious prejudice. . . . In each instance, it is racial discrimination, plain and simple."

Justice Scalia was equally forceful in calling for the end of recognizing race in public policy: "Government can never have a 'compelling interest' in discriminating on the basis of race in order to 'make up' for past racial discrimination in the opposite direction. . . . under our Constitution, there can be no such thing as either a creditor or a debtor race. That concept is alien to the Constitution's focus upon the individual . . . . To pursue the concept of racial entitlement—even for the most admirable and benign of purposes—is to reinforce and preserve for future mischief the way of thinking that produced race slavery, race privilege and race hatred. In the eyes of government, we are just one race here. It is American."

Even Justice Scalia did not go far enough. The race we all are is human.

———

"Randy, we have to go back."

"I'm done with this case. I just want to work."

"You may want to quit, but this is our mission. This is what we are."

"*I've* had enough. This is what *you* are. You and your Val's Fucking Crusade."

———

Our Supreme Court ruling came during Bill Clinton's months-long review of over 160 federal race preference programs. I hoped our decision would cause him to scrap the review and issue a blanket statement ending race preferences, or at least dramatically limit them. A political realist, he had been nudging to the center on topics such as balancing the budget and school prayer. Instead, one month after Adarand v. Peña was decided, he issued his "Mend it, don't end it" stance, and by executive order reaffirmed the principle of affirmative action across the country. He told all of his agencies that government preference programs would continue, but needed to comply with four new provisions: no quotas, no preferences for unqualified people, no reverse discrimination, and no continuation once a program's purpose has been met.

In reality, this did nothing more than make agencies create cosmetic and transparent adjustments, in effect changing the rules while the game was being played. Those rule changes complicated matters for our team.

"It's messy," said Todd. "The administration keeps squirming, throwing up delaying tactics, doing all they can to avoid seeing us in the courtroom."

"What else do you need from us?" I asked. Todd had already spent even more time with Randy confirming the role that government bribes continued to play in Adarand losing business.

"Nothing yet. They are asking for more time—six months more—to find examples of discrimination. Randy and I have done enough talking to the other companies to know that the feds won't find what they want, no matter how many more depositions they take. And we have a good district judge. Kane. He's not putting up with their delays. But even speeding things along, it will still be months."

In those months, progress occurred in California, where Ward Connerly was making a difference. A University of California Regent, he had led a bitter struggle to eliminate race preferences in school admissions, state contracting, and public employment. In the face of enduring and vociferous prejudice, Connerly spearheaded the fight to pass Proposition 209, an affirmative action killer.

And won.

On November 5, the California voters amended their state constitution with this straightforward text: "The state shall not discriminate against, or grant preferential treatment to, any individual or group on the basis of race, sex, color, ethnicity, or national origin in the operation of public employment, public education, or public contracting."

While we were fighting on the national stage to change federal laws, Proposition 209 was to become the model at the local level to get government out of the race-preference business. In time, Ward's beachhead legislation would become the model for numerous states, including Colorado.

But that was still a decade away.

On Dec 20, 1996, we appeared before District Judge John Kane. An ally in procedure—he had expedited this appearance over voluminous objections—he kept his biases on the case merits well concealed.

Only a short time into the proceedings, the U.S. Attorney shocked the court with his assertion. "Your Honor, we conducted depositions all over Colorado, and they show that there is racism in the contracting industry statewide."

Perry and Todd looked at each other. All four eyebrows went up.

"These contractors will not hire a minority unless the government forces them to do it. All of those contractors said the only reason they ever give a job to a minority subcontractor is because of these preferences. That's the kind of racism that exists out there."

Perry shot to his feet. "Your Honor, that is a lie."

He leaned over to Todd and whispered, "Is he telling the truth? Is there any fact in this at all?"

Todd was immediate, "None." He and Randy had put enough hours and miles together to know.

"Are you sure? I'm going out on a limb here."

"Absolutely."

Perry turned back to the microphone and to Judge Kane. "Your honor, that is a lie; it's a damnable lie. I will step away from the microphone and I will allow counsel to point to the record where anyone said that they would not award a contract to a qualified minority bid, because it doesn't exist."

And he stepped back.

Nothing else mattered in the case.

———

"I need to practice looking up," I said to my son.

The Reflecting Pool on Washington D.C.'s National Mall is over a third of a mile long, connecting the Lincoln Memorial on the west to the current site of the World War II Memorial on its east. But in 1997, with the World War II Memorial still years from completion, that east expanse offered not solemnity but rest. After a long morning of museums, including an extended stop at The Star-Spangled Banner, Ted and

I had one stroll remaining against the chill wind of a February afternoon. I used it to practice.

"It's Newt Gingrich. And Oliver North, and lots of others. I can't just read this speech," I said. Not at the Mayflower Hotel, not to honor Ward Connerly. Three weeks prior, Perry Pendley asked me to speak at the Lincoln Leadership Awards, passing on an invitation from House Speaker Gingrich.

"Let's start walking while you read," Ted said. "That way if you look down too much you'll probably land in the pool."

We walked west, toward the Lincoln Memorial, and I read. "In August 1989, the small family business that my husband Randy and I started lost yet another Federal highway subcontract on which we had submitted the lowest bid."

Ted watched me practice simultaneous oration and walking. I watched Lincoln grow larger with each paragraph.

Ted coached. "You're sounding good. I can tell you mean it. Don't forget to look up."

I found my place in the text. "I was told many times that we should be certified as a women-business-enterprise, and so qualify for our piece of the quota pie. I refused to do that because I believe quotas are wrong."

We walked towards the setting sun, towards the Great Emancipator. I spoke and walked and felt every word, summoning the proper authenticity for an event to be held on Lincoln's birthday.

Ted said, "Look up."

I looked up. ". . . we will not pass racial guilt along like a baton, from our generation to the next."

We walked up the broad steps, only a few words remaining in my prepared text. I left the navigation to Ted, my arm hooked in his, but my thoughts on the evening to follow.

"Look up."

". . . and we thank you on behalf of our children, Kendra and Ted. God bless you."

"Now look around."

I turned.

"Look where you are standing."

The Washington Monument seen past the Reflecting Pool is the same vista I saw on my tiny set, in fuzzy grays, when I was eight. I remembered the crowds filling the mall, surrounding the shallow water, and standing together for one message: character, not color.

Ted and I returned to the same spot six years later, soon after Coretta Scott King dedicated a new inscription there on the fortieth anniversary of her husband's most famous speech.

Newly etched in the polished pink and black granite underfoot, dim and subtle for not being painted, eighteen steps below Lincoln's statue, were the following words:

I HAVE A DREAM

MARTIN LUTHER KING, JR.

THE MARCH ON WASHINGTON

FOR JOBS AND FREEDOM

AUGUST 28, 1963

We're getting closer, Dr. King. We're getting closer.

———

Inspired by the success of Ward Connerly's Proposition 209 ballot initiative, Colorado lawmakers attempted to pass a similar bill through the legislature. When House Bill 1299, the "Equal Opportunity Act of 1997" came to the state senate for committee hearings in March, one month after my Lincoln Awards speech, I stood in support. Alongside me were Perry Pendley and long-time family friends Ray Hart, black appraiser, and Jeff Buerger, rugged cowboy.

The Supreme Court Chamber—chosen for its capacity—was nonetheless packed, standing room only for hours. The printed list of citizens signed to speak on the bill included only four in support: Colorado's Attorney General Gale Norton, and my cadre, the three amigos. "NAACP" appended many names on the list.

After an hour of testimony supporting race preferences, Perry took the microphone. Against the room's sentiment even his cogency found little purchase. "The question is not," he testified, "'Will racial discrimination by private individuals when in violation of the law be permitted?' It will not be permitted. The question really ought to be, 'How long will *government* continue to do what we tell private individuals they can never do, which is make decisions on the basis of race?'"

An hour after Perry spoke, and following another half-dozen race hustlers, Nicole Retland broke my heart.

Petite, composed, pretty, and black, she sat before the panel and lowered the microphone. "My name is Nicole Retland. I am a 7th-grader in the IB program at Hamilton Middle School, and an honor roll student. I plan to attend college and go on to medical school."

This eloquent and accomplished young lady had the world before her. With her poise and drive she represented the best of our youth's promise.

"—but without affirmative action my opportunities may not be the same as my Caucasian peers. My grandparents and parents have benefited from affirmative action. My grandparents struggled that I too may have better opportunities and not be judged by the color of my skin, but by my qualifications."

But affirmative action means just the opposite of that. Instead of seeing your qualifications, future classmates and workmates will wonder if skin color is the reason for your progress. As long as affirmative action is in place, you'll never be judged solely on your qualifications, and you'll never know the legitimate esteem that comes from advancing in a color-blind environment.

After another hour of people testifying that the system owed them something, I had my chance to rebut, decrying the injustice of a spoils system based on race and sex. Many watched closely, most with squints and set jaws. Ray followed me, a man so dear to my family that my father calls him his other son, and my brothers and I all call him our other brother.

From their outcry just after he began, it was apparent the crowd expected him to be another preference seeker. Ray's invocation of Dr. Martin Luther King, with "Sometimes silence is betrayal," provoked a cry of "Traitor!" from a mass near the door, suddenly a mob of anonymity. Over the years Ray had told us enough stories of verbal abuse (although usually from redneck whitey) that we knew his "sticks and stones" armor to be strong.

Our last lone ranger pressed on. "Affirmative action is broken. It has outlived its usefulness." The other speakers dissented.

"There is a certain stigma." The crowd dissented.

"We've lost our pride." The blacks dissented.

Ray rejoined us: my cowboy, my lawyer, my black brother, and me. We had been resisting the crowd's flow, holding our ground inside the chambers, isolated advocates and fully outnumbered. But there were no more speakers on our behalf, and a queue of twenty more in opposition milled at demonstration ready, their indignation and sense of entitlement having spilled into the chamber as catcalls during Ray's time at the microphone.

We trickled into the hall, now its own echo chamber: Ray and Jeff first; I followed; Perry was caught in the net of bodies. I drew a flash crowd—eight women, all Hispanic, all angry. All loud.

"Traitor!" One behind me shouted.

That word again. As if by standing for self-reliance I had violated some women's code of solidarity in subjugation.

Then from every side: "Women deserve better than you! You're a traitor to your gender! You don't represent *any* of us!"

I certainly didn't. Their only strength was in numbers and in embracing their weakness, their values polluted by an incestuous dependency on handouts and set-asides. I had had enough. My breath came fast in the same way it had when Grandpa Ted demanded that I not talk to my black friend Gary, the same way it had when I woke to a burning cross in Jim Crow Louisiana. This was wrong. Too wrong for pity.

I wheeled on my heels like standing in a saddle, taller than myself, and looked each in the eye. "I'm really sorry for all of you that you don't believe enough in yourself. When you want to grow up and be real women, let me know, because real women don't have to use government programs to show they're worthy."

During their passing moment of surprise, this perplexing violation of their code, commotion further down the hall rose to an angry spike. I elbowed past their resurging resentment to close on Jeff, his stance wary, where beyond him a funnel of incoming people filled the capitol hall—save for a clearing near the door, ringed like a schoolyard confrontation.

Ray stood at its center, his egress blocked.

Never in all the high-country brawls and schoolyard slap-fights had I heard so many shouts of "Nigger!" and "Uncle Tom!" and "Nigger!" some more. All from black men, four of whom converged on Ray, the closest with chin high, chest out, palms upturned. His voice thick with Black Pride: "What the fuck are you—Clarence Thomas' poster boy?"

I saw Jeff tense. He was closer to Ray than I was, but still yards away from the confrontation. His fists clenched and his weight shifted forward, a college athlete's ready stance.

Ray surveyed his aggressor, appraised his demeanor, evaluated his worth. He said, "I don't think you need to step too much closer to me." I had never heard Ray's *don't fuck with me* tone, a resolution backed by imminent threat. Its message could not have been clearer, not to the crowd who quieted, sensing volatility, nor to the Alpha Negro, who invited it.

One step further into Ray's space, the race thug spat his dominance: "You. My. Nigger." A claim of ownership, not fellowship.

On the ranch, lesser men fought over half a bottle of skid-row hooch or a pack of mislaid chaw. My friend Ray was not a lesser man.

"Get . . . out of my way," from him was enough.

Together Jeff and I closed on Ray as he stepped towards the narrow clearing now before him—a parted Black Sea likely to crash back in momentarily. The two of us linked Ray's arms, one on each side, and hastened to the exit, taunts ringing behind.

Not every philosophical opponent heckled. Some, even in the same halls we had just left, merely misunderstood ends and means.

Colorado Senate Republican patriarch Ray Powers served over twenty years in the state legislature, a gentleman leader and dealmaker. Like my dad, he left school as a teen to run his family's ranch, the Powers' dairy farm in eastern Colorado Springs. I thought he would understand the value of hard work, having spent decades raising cattle before entering politics.

At the state capitol, trying to gain the support of any legislator who would listen, I found him in his office, and explained our case. "Gee, Val. What's the problem?" he said, with fractionally too much condescension. "Just play the game. The company is in your name; you hold most of the stock. Apply for the DBE status and get those contracts based on gender."

I was insulted. "DBE. Listen to the words. *Disadvantaged* business enterprise. I'm not disadvantaged, and I won't claim it. What about my brains? My talent? My competitive spirit?"

The Republican icon from my city took off his glasses and looked me straight in the eye. "I've been here a long time. I'm telling you it's not worth the fight. Play the game."

"I thought you would understand," I said. "I do payroll and clean the office. I'm not out pounding in posts. I'm a director, but I work mostly from home. I can't represent that I'm at the office every day, or on the trucks every day. Randy does that."

His shrug ended the conversation. Closing the door I recalled one of my proudest moments as a parent. My daughter, Kendra, excelled at hockey throughout high school—too much for the girls her age: their leagues presented no challenge for her talent and aggression.

When the head coach weighed her application for the boys' division, he suggested she play down a level. "These boys are sixteen and seventeen," he said, sizing her up. "You'll get smashed. We'll put you in bantam."

"No," she said, dismissing the opportunity to play against boys no smaller but a year or two younger than she was. "I'll play my age. Just because I'm a girl doesn't give me a right to cheat the system."

Coach looked at me, his eyebrows suggesting tears and injuries. "You heard her," I said.

No pink saddles on the ranch. No pink helmets on the rink.

Exiting the capitol, I considered the message we send to our daughters and our granddaughters when we say, "You get a preference because you're a girl," how it robs a parent of the chance to tell her child, as I did, how proud I was of her, and how it demeans a girl to play along with a system that expects less because of her gender.

I will not perpetuate such slurs on half the human race.

———

On June 2, 1997, almost two years after the case was remanded from the Supreme Court, Colorado District Court Judge John Kane ruled that the set-asides we initially opposed, eight years prior, were, under the new strict scrutiny standard, unconstitutional. He stopped the minority preference program cold. Dead. Done.

Finally we could just get to work.

Eleven weeks later the United States appealed Kane's ruling.

Walt Gallagher, ranch hand, on hay stacker, high above the vermin

CHAPTER ELEVEN

Vermin in the Dark

"I certify that I am socially disadvantaged."

RANDY PECH

My daughter walked out on us the day she turned eighteen. She literally walked. She would have driven away, but the Angry White Male had just slashed her tires.

"You're eighteen now. Show some manners," said Randy, when Kendra used a biscuit to scoop the last of her birthday pot roast. On this Colorado summer evening we were dining outside, a cool breeze and panoramic view from the deck our reward for living miles from town.

This again. I saw Kendra's head shake, her jaw clench, her eyes roll.

"Val, look at how she is. She eats like a pig." Randy had found another trivial slight to his sensibilities, another opportunity to blanket the occasion with his special brand of holiday cheer. For years now, no birthday had gone unspoiled, no holiday remained pristine; instead Randy found ways to humiliate his children, to suck the joy out of an occasion, leaving instead his signature pout and the discomfort of a family too worn down to combat his ego.

"Stop it, Randy, she—" I said.

"It's disrespectful. Other kids don't act like that." His ire was up and his words came faster. We could tell that this tirade was just getting started. "She doesn't appreciate anything, the little piggy." Like the foosball table he bought her after shoving her down the stairs.

Kendra pushed herself back from the remains of our *al fresco* dinner. "I'm leaving," she said, standing. "I am eighteen, just like you said, and I don't have to hear your shit any more."

"Sit down," said Randy. "You don't know how good you have it."

"I'm done. I'm an adult with my own car. You can't stop me now." Kendra stepped inside and grabbed her keys from the counter. "I don't have to live here. I don't have to be around *you* any more."

"You are not leaving!" Randy leapt to his feet and snatched her keys. She sighed and walked away. He flashed me his "that's how you handle children" look, one that evaporated moments later when Kendra returned with her spare keys, and strode to the garage hallway.

This time he muscled past her at a run. "No, you won't!" he shouted, storming into the garage.

I was behind them both, Kendra and I jostling to get past the door he momentarily tried to close behind himself. "Stop! Just leave her alone!" I yelled. "Let her go!"

Randy didn't stop. Instead he found a screwdriver, gave it a good once over for suitability, and drove it into the sidewall of the right front tire. Then the left front, the left rear, and the right rear, a methodical stalking parade of ownership and control. "Now you're not leaving," he said, beaming, as he walked back inside.

An hour later I saw Kendra from my bedroom window. As I packed my bag upstairs, she walked away from our house, backpack over one shoulder, phone in the other hand, her thumb working the buttons.

I gave her a good head start.

Later, with my suitcase in hand, I found Randy hunched over his computer. "I can't be around this," I told him. "I'm leaving."

"Whatever. The ungrateful brat does not deserve that car. And you'll be back."

He was right.

———

"It won't do you much good just to trap the mice you got now," said Walt Gallagher, strolling the hay barn with me twenty-five years earlier. "More just keep coming back. They're clever, and there's lots of 'em."

We kept bigger vermin at bay with rifles and fence. Relentless, tiny pests needed something else.

"Poison's good, but mostly, you need cats. You need something active, with teeth."

Slippery federal and state lawmakers scurried and shuffled, tweaking programs, renaming initiatives, undertaking "disparity studies," and generally doing every thing to avoid complying with the Supreme- and District-court decisions that came from our efforts. Through it all they kept scores of minority contract preferences fundamentally intact, like too many mice.

Judge Kane had declared the federal DBE rules unconstitutional, and yet Colorado still relied on those for guidance when the state funneled federal dollars through its contracting programs. So we filed a second suit, this time to stop Governor Romer from perpetuating the cycle of race preferences.

Our aim was to unleash another cat, with teeth.

But it turned on us.

In normal defense of a suit against a state, its Attorney General defends the state's position; however, Gale Norton had more principle than that. As the only other person to speak alongside the three amigos on behalf of HB 1299, she knew the flaws in Colorado's contracting rules, even calling them "indefensible." Governor Romer, undeterred, selected outside counsel.

Former Colorado Supreme Court Justice Jean Dubofsky, the first woman appointed to that office, argued for the state. She insisted that Colorado had adopted new rules, that they hadn't used the federal race-based guidelines that Judge Kane—the judge we were again in front of—had recently ruled unconstitutional. She asserted that Colorado had a newer, fairer model, one that relied not on race, but on "social disadvantage," based upon the effects of racial, ethnic, or gender discrimination.

Kane seized upon the concept of "social disadvantage" and found a loophole in Dubrofsky's claims, one neither side anticipated.

He insisted that because Adarand had lost so many contracts for being the wrong race, those years of discrimination against us made us socially disadvantaged as well. And because we were disadvantaged, we could no longer claim injury from the DBE rules in place. Kane found that the state regulations for DBE certification could remain, because, as he saw it, he had just rendered them meaningless. Now everyone could claim social disadvantage: blacks for being black, and whites for being not black.

In the Denver sunlight afterwards, once outside Kane's Federal District Court, I vented my frustration. "Did I hear that right? Did he just say that we have to become a DBE company?"

"We don't have to, but he said we can." The two lawyers measured out only a few words, and slowly, pondering the implications.

"Well, I won't do it!" I said. "How many times do I have to say we are not disadvantaged?"

"But his ruling actually said that you were, specifically, discriminated against. All those denied contracts made you socially disadvantaged."

I was angrier than at any time in our legal struggle. The system itself had created an upside-down logic naming everyone equally unequal: a bizarre, infuriating Venn diagram with every section labeled "disadvantaged" and no section labeled "judged on individual merit."

"Wait a minute! It's more than that." I was angry at the appalling concept of universal disadvantage, but just as worried about the consequences. "If we become a DBE company, won't that hurt our standing on the federal level? On our primary case?"

Todd puzzled through the implications. "I think Val's right." He turned to me. "We need to put you on legal staff."

Kane was supposed to rule on our injunction, unleashing one more cat with teeth against the scurrying, insidious race preference programs. Instead, in what he may have thought was a roundabout success, he altered the entire landscape, and put ideas in Randy's head. Bad ideas.

———

"All I have to do is check a box that says I've been discriminated against." Randy had his pen in hand.

"I hate those boxes."

"It's not like I want to become a member of the program, but you heard Judge Kane. We'll get exactly what we want if Colorado will stop making its decisions based on race."

"That is not at all what I want. The rules are all still broken and this won't fix them."

"The only way to change it is from within. If all of us are DBEs, it's the same as none of us being DBEs."

"It's not the same. Don't check the box. Don't sign it."

This is what Randy Pech signed: "I certify that I am socially disadvantaged because I have been subjected to racial or ethnic prejudice or cultural bias, or have suffered the effects of discrimination, because of my identity as a member of one or more of the groups identified above, without regard to my individual qualities."

With that signature, he added years to our legal marathon.

———

Randy worked hard and made good money, so sending Ted to Academy of Art College was no hardship. Halfway through his first school year, our son asked for money. He was supposed to; that was Randy's promise when we drove Ted to San Francisco: "You concentrate on school. I'll take care of your expenses."

Ted had made nearly $7000 working on Adarand's crew the past two summers, punching holes in I-beams, pounding posts, fork-lifting concrete barriers into place—enough for tuition and for moving in. Not enough for a year in San Francisco.

But when Ted first called for money, Randy reneged. "Where's all the money you had in your bank account?" he barked into the phone. The tone was familiar, the same one he used with me every Wednesday night when we discussed family finances. On the other end of the line, Ted would be as powerless as I had become, worn out from too many of the same battles over too many of the same topics. We needed reinforcements. We needed a fighter.

I called Mom.

The next day, Randy came home to: "What's this I hear about not giving your son money for food and supplies and everything else?" Preliminary niceties were not among Mother's social graces.

Niceties of any kind were not among Randy's social graces. "He burns through it too fast," he said. "Ted needs to learn to not spend so much."

"Spend so much? What the hell's that in the driveway?" My mother jerked a thumb over her shoulder. New off the showroom floor gleamed a two-door SLK-class silver convertible roadster, Randy's kind of shiny. "You have enough money for a goddamn Mercedes-Benz, but you don't have enough money for your boy to eat?"

Randy tried to shuffle past Alta. His choices for any confrontation were to sulk or shout, and he had not yet worked up a shouting ire.

She said, "What kind of parent doesn't help his children? Jack and I helped every one of our kids get started out."

He said, "Well nobody helped me. I built Adarand on my own."

Randy's memory of how the business started, of how his parents and sister gave him start-up money, must have failed, but his temper leapt to attention when obliged to defend his own constructed story. Now there would be shouting instead of sulking.

She raised her voice. "It's what you do, you help your children."

He raised his voice. "That's ridiculous. When's he going to learn the value of hard work?"

She got louder. "Right now! He's working now instead of going to classes because he can't afford to eat!"

Nobody ever talked back to Randy. I would pay for this later.

He got louder. "He had plenty of money. He's not being smart with it. You need to mind your own fucking business."

She yelled, "My family is my business."

He yelled, "You don't come in *my* house and tell me what to do with *my* son."

She turned on her heel and said, "I expect I won't be coming to your house at all."

I found ways to route money through Alta to Ted. This felt too much like hoarding getaway money the way I had hidden a few hundred dollars in my back pocket eighteen years earlier and 250 miles north of where Ted was now. I hoped my pockets were big enough.

———

Randy's signature acknowledging social disadvantage derailed our original case. Three years prior, the Supreme Court had told the Denver District Court to re-examine the DBE rules under the tighter strict scrutiny standards. One year prior, District Judge Kane did so, and admitted that those original rules were no longer constitutional. The

United States appealed Kane's ruling, clearing the path for another trip for all of us back through the appellate Circuit Court.

Except we couldn't continue. Not for lack of funds or legal expertise, or even will—we couldn't continue because with Randy's signature we were no longer injured by the original rules designating disadvantage. No longer suffering discrimination in getting contracts, we lost our standing, according the US's motion to dismiss. Without standing, our entire argument was moot, they claimed—rendered meaningless and superseded by circumstance. And based on that, the Tenth Circuit set aside Kane's ruling, solely because the case was moot, not on its merits.

"I told you so."

"I just want to work."

Regaining our standing entailed a circuitous, slippery, arcane two-year detour, which landed our case, but not our physical presence, in the Supreme Court for a second time. Along the way the landscape changed even further: We let our DBE status lapse, and the state and federal DBE rules continued to shift.

When our petition for cert finally reached the Supreme Court, they took quick notice and unanimously restored our standing with a *per curiam* decision—one that is unanimous and unsigned. The Supreme Court ruled without ever asking us to appear in person. In doing so they overturned the Tenth Circuit's decision that our case was moot, and remanded it back for consideration on the merits.

Perry Pendley put the Supreme's action in perspective. "There are three things that can happen to a Supreme Court case," he said. "The first is most common, it's what happened to us five years ago: You file a petition. There's an opposition, a reply, cert's granted. You have brief, you have arguments, and you get a ruling."

Years of struggle compressed into seven shorthand steps.

"The second case is you file a petition, opposition, reply. And then the Supreme Court, based only on these—no arguments—grants, reverses, and remands. That is what it just did."

But not often. The Highest Court settles fewer than ten cases per year with a *per curiam* opinion like ours.

"The third case is you can have a petition, opposition, reply, cert's granted, brief, argue. But then . . . dismissed as improvidently granted. You get a 'dig,' it's an acronym."

"You said 'dismissed.' It's thrown out?"

"Oh yes. After you argue, the Court says that it should never have granted cert in the first place. The dig is a terrible thing," he said. "But it's very rare. It happens maybe only once a term. Maybe less. Not worth worrying about."

———

After its journey up to the Supreme Court, our case landed back down in the lap of Circuit Court Judge Carlos Lucero, the first Hispanic to sit on the Tenth Circuit, and a Clinton appointee. The same judge who dismissed our case as moot when we called Adarand a DBE company was now directed to judge the case on its merits instead of on our standing.

It seemed he was all too happy to rule against us a second time. I imagined him thinking, as he issued his opinion, "You're going to make me judge this after all? Fine then. We put window dressing on the rules so they are now constitutional even with your new strict scrutiny standards. You lose again. So there." My internal dialogue did not conform to the highest standards of jurisprudence.

Square One.

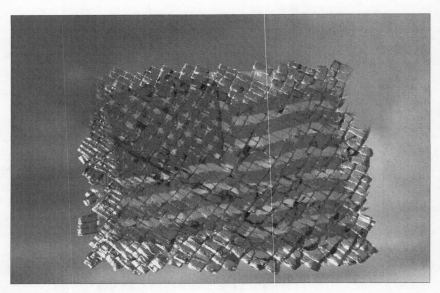

I saved the flag!

I Believe

"Freedom itself was attacked this morning by a faceless coward, and freedom will be defended."

PRESIDENT GEORGE W. BUSH, SEPTEMBER 11, 2001

The struggle for equal treatment is a marathon. First for those whose skin was so dark that their rights were trampled for hundreds of years, then for those whose skin was so light that they were damaged by the excesses of overcorrecting.

In 1995 the Supreme Court remanded our case back to lower courts to determine whether the DBE program was still constitutional once the strict scrutiny standard was applied. The Colorado District Court had decided that it was not, that the contracting spoils system violated the law. Having failed to dissuade us with its detours on mootness and standing, the Tenth Circuit Court—Judge Lucero—overturned the District's ruling.

The first time we filed for a writ of certiorari, we crossed our fingers and knew that our chances were slim. This time when Mountain States filed, we fully expected cert to be granted. The Supreme Court had sent this case down a six-year rabbit hole when they remanded it instead of deciding it in 1995. We felt as if we had dutifully followed the High Court's instructions to apply the new standard in the proper venue, and imagined they were just waiting for the day when the case would land back in their jurisdiction.

A third appearance at the Supreme Court is almost unprecedented for any litigant, but we felt as if they had invited us back. They must have thought so too. Writ for our third appearance was granted on March 26, 2001.

Government-sponsored bias was not only rampant, but increasing, and we were once again poised to abolish it. As I told the National Press Club seven months later, on the eve of our oral arguments, "Despite legislative and courtroom mandates, neither Congress nor the executive branch have abandoned their use of racial preferences. Even in our state, the DOT recently announced an aggressive effort to increase its goals for minority and female owned companies."

Our job was getting no easier.

But time was slipping away. Every month that passed made reconsideration of our original case just a little less meaningful as new programs, even if new in name only, replaced the old ones. And every month that passed made life at home a little less tolerable. There, Wednesdays had devolved into a ritual power play, one I came to think of as my "Wednesday night beating," with Randy scrutinizing every credit card receipt and check register entry.

"You paid too much for milk," he said. The next week it was gas. Utilities the next. Wednesday after Wednesday, all through 2001. Through June and July and August and Sep—.

And then every single thing changed.

———

September 11, 2001. Four airliners became death.

———

On a June morning in 1968, ranch bard and rogue Gary McMahan burst in on our camp breakfast, breathless and grim. "Another one's been shot."

That was Bobby Kennedy, killed the midnight prior in California. In spring of that year, Martin Luther King had been gunned down. All year long, the year following the Summer of Love, the Vietnam War dominated television coverage, casualty on top of carnage on top of atrocity.

But even those deaths were spread out over months. Not minutes.

———

The smoke and dust would last for days, but the images of collapse are permanently seared on our nation's psyche. I remembered other private images, images from a time I almost died.

1972. Raining. Night. Gary McMahan had spent weeks building an earthen dam to reroute and capture the summer's excess rain. As a bonus, the dam created a shortcut to the Williams Fork Reservoir, across a new and unfamiliar route.

The dam had not yet been topped with roadfill for traction and drainage. Instead, the surface comprised what his earth-moving had excavated: very little silt and sand, very much clay. Wet clay. But I was in too much of a hurry, and too cocky behind the wheel.

One slip on the new surface, and then a failure of overcorrecting: a slide the opposite way and a helpless skid sideways off the embankment. The bottom dropped from underneath my Jeep Wagoneer and suddenly I rolled, side over side.

I gripped the wheel with both hands. "Oh God." Not a startled panic, but more of a slow-motion divine summoning, the construction of a spiritual roll cage, given shape by my faith and spine by my God. I believe. I believe.

Behind me inside the car, flashing in the rear-view mirror, my cargo of laundry, fresh clothes for a sharp appearance at the Trading Post tomorrow, tumbled as if in a giant dryer. Outside, my twin headlight beams spun through sprays of mud and rain, the embankment tumbling by. I sat motionless, hands at ten and two, as the world rolled around me.

I believe.

The vehicle jolted to a stop on its passenger side.

I recall crawling out the driver's side window. Gary McMahan found me bedraggled and muddy, running for home, not a scratch on me.

When we returned the next morning, my laundry was strewn across shrubs and mud, on the slope and at the base of the dam. Every window in the Wagoneer was missing, the shattered fragments embedded in the mud underfoot. One larger piece of the rear window glistened on the ground, its small, spiderwebbed, granular chunks held together by a sticker I had on the back window. A sticker of an American flag.

On the driver's side, the Jeep's roof was smashed all the way down to the steering wheel.

I saved the flag.

———

Our skies were silent in the days following the attacks, an uncomfortable aerial paralysis. The stillness disquieted me. On the ground, in my own tiny sphere, I determined to celebrate movement instead.

I had for years coached a competitive jazz dance team. Ever since a fall in college ended my personal gymnastics and dance aspirations, I had coached the Cheyenne Mountain High School dance team to perennial success as Colorado's top-scoring 4A performers. Coaching dance was better than showing cattle. When girls kick, they leave smiles, not scars.

Coaching the team had been my escape from work, from Randy, and from the legal odyssey—an opportunity to help girls grow their talent along with their character, meshing self-expression with self-respect in a realm where what mattered was results, not privilege. "Anybody can teach you to dance," I told them. "It's far more important to be strong young women."

Our annual fundraiser was scheduled for September 27, a performance already rehearsed for months. And then the towers fell.

Amid the shock, and with smoke still billowing from the wreckage, we channeled heartbreak and anger into a new direction. We had planned pink and black. We changed to red, white, and blue. Instead of limiting the performance to only our eighteen dancers, I invited coaches from around the state to join us—adding eighty more. We revamped the entire production to include singers and dramatic readings. We planned the "Dance for Freedom."

Introducing the performance to a packed house that night, I reminded the tearful crowd that freedom is not free, and suggested that we never take our freedoms for granted. From the rubble American citizens would rise up in defiance, as our dancers would tonight, celebrating freedom.

Our dance team's display case held awards from years of success, each prize given to us a token of a job well done. But for the "Dance for Freedom," we did not receive a thing in recognition. Instead we gave it. With the team beside me, we performed our most important act ever when we handed a check to the American Red Cross.

———

A week later our legal team headed to DC.

While we did our small part in Colorado, George Bush and Congress rushed to strengthen security nationwide, capitalizing on a rare moment of legislative unity.

On October 24 the USA PATRIOT Act passed the House by a 5-to-1 margin.

On October 25 it passed the Senate on a 98-to-1 vote.

On October 26 George Bush signed it into law. Might a country so unified in purpose see that our similarities as Americans ought to be recognized, instead of our differences in melanin?

On that day an external threat closed the Supreme Court building. On the next, we arrived in Washington, D.C., the city where two postal workers had just died from anthrax.

I had looked forward to the massive bronze doors, the grand entrance hall, and the courtroom itself, both so small and so large. I had anticipated the reverence and weight of the institution, made real in marble and velvet. I had wanted to breathe the air of the courtroom again.

But this time, the atmosphere was poisoned. Literally. Three people were dead nationwide and a dozen hospitalized from *Bacillus anthrasis*, and the count of anthrax hot spots was climbing daily, amid a broad tension of barely contained panic. Poison had been routed through mail centers in New York, Congress, the White House, the State Department, and the Supreme Court.

Over the next months five people would die to the virus, and it would take nine years for the FBI to finally close the case, with its primary suspect having committed suicide two years prior. But at the time, two days before our scheduled arguments, we all knew little, except that the building was closed, that the justices were being administered the antibiotic ciprofloxacin as a precaution, and that our case would be moved.

For the first time since its opening sixty-six years ago, the Supreme Court building was shut down for arguments. Cases this week were heard at the nearby E. Barrett Prettyman Federal Courthouse. That structure housed the District Court and the Circuit Court of Appeals for the District of Columbia, but capacity and security were at an all-time high. As a result, almost none of the Adarand supporters would be able to attend the oral arguments.

Instead, we could gather somewhere only if we paid for the privilege.

———

"No!" Randy barked. "We've already spent enough money. I'm not feeding that crowd, too."

"We need to thank those few allies who have stood by us," I said. "The least we can do is buy them dinner."

"Nope. Half that room will be lawyers anyway. They all have wallets."

"You can stay here. I'm going, and I'm paying."

I hosted our allies at the Hard Times Cafe, in Alexandria, Virginia: a peanuts-on-the-floor, Colorado-in-DC kind of real. No airs. About twenty friends and supporters had joined us, including brothers Ed and Clair and their wives Susie and Deb, Joe Nance and his new bride Jennifer, Ward Connerly, and the Mountain States Legal Team.

Outside, on the day before Halloween, it was brisk autumn: trees celebrating in maroons and marigolds. Inside, we celebrated the journey. I knew this would be our last appearance at the Supreme Court. Regardless of the outcome, this team had already been through fire together, and no cause would be enough to ask them back. After this we would let others follow the roads we paved. Tonight was for gratitude.

As we gathered in the reserved room upstairs, I handed out a selection of insights I had prepared, called "I Believe." Among its watchwords:

I believe in the supreme worth of the individual.

I believe that a noble endeavor once exposed never dies.

I believe in America, because we have great dreams, and the opportunity to make those dreams come true.

Our venue, Hard Times, seemed appropriate, its name reflecting not only our twelve-year journey here, but the recent threats as well, terrorist assaults exploiting both technology and biology.

"Thank you, my fellow warriors . . . "

I was seasoned. Twelve years in the breach gave me confidence—

not that we would win, but in myself and the mission. Confidence to fight big fights.

"The message we deliver to the Supreme Court is simple: preferential treatment and discrimination are two sides of the same coin—and that coin is illegal tender in a nation that was founded upon the precept that all are created equal."

Equal justice under law is the simplest of ideas. Achieving it is the hardest of struggles.

Randy scowled at the menu and the price of chili dogs.

———

American Airlines flight 77, the terrorist bomb that crashed into the Pentagon, killed 125 people on the ground and all 64 people on board: 6 crew, 5 murderers, and 53 passengers. Among the passengers was Barbara Olson, a lawyer who had worked with Clarence Thomas when he chaired the Equal Employment Opportunity Commission, and who defended him at his Senate confirmation hearings. She led the Travelgate and Filegate investigations against the Clinton administration, and was a frequent commentator on CNN and Fox News.

During the hijacking, Barbara Olson made two calls to her husband, reporting that she and the other passengers had been herded into the back of the plane, and that the hijackers had box cutters and knives. Less than ten minutes later, at a speed of 530 mph, her airliner crashed into the west side of the Pentagon and through the three outermost of the building's five rings. She was on her way to film Bill Maher's *Politically Incorrect*.

Barbara Olson had planned to fly to Los Angeles on Monday, September 10, but instead stayed one more day to have breakfast with her husband for his birthday. Her husband, Ted Olson, turned 61 on September 11, 2001, the day his wife and nearly 3000 others were slain. Less than two months later, on Halloween, he finally returned to work, making his first appearance before the Supreme Court since his wife's murder.

Ted Olson, the United States Solicitor General, was arguing against us.

The Supreme Court always shows deference to the Solicitor General, the government's chief advocate in the Court, and because of its importance, the role is commonly called the "Tenth Justice." The nine robed justices could not be blind to feelings for the man they saw most often arguing before them.

On this day, would that deference be more? Would it be sympathy? How could it not?

———

Six years prior, the oral arguments had a different tenor. Then, the same nine justices challenged the essence of the suit, but this time they haggled not over what role race should play in making contracting fair or legal, but over what case Perry was arguing.

Later Perry told me that he knew he was in trouble fifteen seconds into his remarks when Chief Justice Rehnquist interrupted him point blank: "Do we simply have a factual dispute here?" Factual disputes are not resolved in the Supreme Court; the Highest Court is not a trier of fact. At best, the Supreme Court remands a case when more fact-finding is needed, a frustrating yo-yo ride we knew all too well. At worst, it's much worse.

Justice Breyer, part of the liberal half of the court, exposed the case's difficulty in an unusually clear and succinct series of questions: "What are we supposed to do?" he asked. "The lower court didn't address the issue you want to raise."

One seldom heard the justices speak such plain language, and even I knew that this court reviewed only those topics directly addressed in the lower courts.

Breyer continued. "So, what is it you suggest we do? Do we send it back to the lower court? Do we dig the whole thing? Do we do something else?"

I hoped it was "something else," because neither of Breyer's first two choices had any appeal to our team. Neither, apparently did they to Justice Kennedy, whose face for this exchange bloomed vivid red. I wondered if he saw his opportunity to issue a ruling diminish as the case seemed to be slipping away.

When Perry finally had the opportunity to address the underlying injustice of the criteria used for race preferences, about the sweeping presumption of inferiority based on skin color, he spoke poetry. "It's ageless in its ability to reach into a person's past. Timeless in its ability to affect their future. And nothing removes the taint from an individual, not winning a Nobel Peace Prize, not election to the U.S. Senate, and not graduating magna cum laude from the Wharton School of Business at the University of Pennsylvania. Nothing removes the taint."

A presumption of inferiority is everlasting.

But instead of being able to spend his time arguing the intrinsic unfairness of the programs as they were being practiced, Perry was forced into an uncomfortable and murky debate on standing, mootness, fact, and scope.

A debate nobody could win.

———

Less than a month after we argued our case, the Supreme Court issued its opinion, again *per curiam*: another unanimous, unsigned opinion. The opinion disappointed us and everyone else who was looking to the Court to take a definitive stand on the inherent unfairness of government-sponsored race preferences.

The opinion issued on November 27, 2001, dismissed our case as improvidently granted. The third result that could happen to a case, the "dig" that Perry Pendley called a "terrible thing," the ruling that is no ruling at all—happened to us. The Supreme Court threw out the case.

It took me some time to puzzle out the opinion's meaning, but like worrying a scab that itches more than it hurts, I dug at it until I understood.

As an appellate court, the Supreme Court rules only whether lower court rulings are constitutional; it is a court of review, not of first view. When it originally granted cert, the Supreme Court understood that we would be challenging only direct Federal programs—no state involvement—such as our initial claim in the San Juan National Forest job. But the Supreme Court ruled that in our Circuit Court appeal, the Tenth Circuit did not address the direct federal programs, but instead addressed only state-administered programs that happened to be funneling federal money. The regulations for state-filtered funds and for direct funds are different.

In essence, the Court said that we briefed and argued something outside the scope of the Circuit Court's decisions, and that our discussion of the direct federal program was impossible for them to adjudicate, since it would have called for them to make decisions of fact. It would have asked them to judge on details of how the direct federal program was being implemented, but on that topic, material facts remained in dispute.

So two things went awry. The Supreme Court had no jurisdiction to resolve those disputed facts, and the direct federal program was not subject to review since it was not the one the Tenth Circuit Court ruled on. For both reasons, despite the case's importance, all nine justices agreed that they were powerless to rule.

And whether with reluctance or relief, out of respect for their institution, they dismissed the case.

———

The fight goes on.

After twelve years, three Supreme Court appearances, countless lower-court decisions, five transportation secretaries, and three presidents, we failed to get to the promised land.

Perhaps the legal team could have been more precise in its arguments, adhering closer to the matters directly addressed at the Tenth Circuit. Perhaps they could have been less tenacious in trying to make the claim that the exact programs in place in 2001 were still the ones unfairly applied to us a dozen years earlier, programs the government was adamant had long since been surpassed by circumstance.

Perhaps our case outlived its initial conditions, but the fact that federal contracting procedures continue to treat people based on skin color attests to the difficulty of getting past our collective white guilt and culture of special privilege. Certainly those sentiments are reinforced with every continuing application of affirmative action in American life.

Even without the fairy tale conclusion, the Adarand case still made important, if only incremental progress. We overturned Metro, the 1990 ruling that set the low baseline of only intermediate scrutiny for federal race programs. Instead, the equal protection treatment established in Croson, but previously applicable only locally, is now in force across the nation: Congress is obliged to apply the strict scrutiny standard just as cities and states are. The federal government gets no special dispensation to discriminate.

And although its value was subtle and hidden deep inside legal arcana, our second Supreme Court victory forced the judiciary to acknowledge that a case does not become irrelevant, or moot, just because those who implement the regulations change the labels in elaborate legal shell games. Shuffling names and deck chairs does not allow agencies the license to avoid their day in court.

What darkens the landscape is that even our substantive rulings are still often ignored. Enforcement of the strict scrutiny standard remains lax, at best. But I hold out hope. I have confidence that we as a country, and nine justices as a body, can, in time, move past institutionalizing the idea of racial inferiority and issue the definitive ruling that race has no place in public policy.

———

I wanted an enduring legal landmark, but until then I would always have a real one, at the Granby homestead, our family's refuge for over a century.

Early December at the ranch is always a time to hang Christmas decorations. Similar festivities at home in Colorado Springs were premature, since Randy and I had just moved to our new country club home the week prior. My mother and I savored the quiet and lightness of having no lawsuit pending for the first time in twelve years.

"I need to thank you for showing me how to take a strong stand," I said from my stepstool at the fireplace, a string of colored lights in hand. "You were never afraid to take on anybody. If I hadn't seen you do that, I could never have persevered through all this."

Alta sipped her ginger ale. Not all nights were scotch with a lemon twist these days. "Aw, it's just second nature to me. I've fought my whole life." On our weathered dining table, she separated ornaments: old, older, and oldest.

"But here's what's strange," I said. "I'm not tired from all that. I'm energized. I feel stronger."

Mounted on the wall above the mantle is a wagon bow, an arced strut that at one time supported the canopy of my great-grandfather's covered wagon. Five remain in our family: this one, one for each of my brothers, and mine. I had not yet thought of any appropriate spot for it in my new house. I tapped the weathered hardwood as I wound holiday lights beneath it.

"Of course you are," my mother said. "The most important fights, those put more into you than they take out. Ornery makes you stronger."

I stepped down to examine my mother's decorations now spread out, a nostalgic array of tradition and distant holidays. "So I shouldn't stop fighting?"

"How do you think I've lasted this long?" she said. "Besides, stick around long enough and you get a chance to correct some things along the way. You might find that what religion doesn't cure, age will."

She grinned, the same way she did when she read me Heidi forty years ago, about a young girl, prospering among the animals and mountains, who became homesick for the Alps when she was trapped in a dreary, faraway city, there to be mistreated by an oppressive taskmaster. Miserably homesick, every single day.

Perhaps I wouldn't decorate the Colorado Springs house after all.

With Bob Beauprez on the steps of the United Stated Capitol

CHAPTER THIRTEEN

Defiance

"All I know is that I will not wash my own underwear!"

ANGRY WHITE MALE

In January, Ward Connerly invited me to participate in a Washington, D.C., summit to hone our message of equality, a message to counter the semantic hijacking of the public debate on race preferences. Randy told me I couldn't go.

"Well, I'm going."

In April, Ward Connerly invited me to Sacramento, to speak at the American Civil Rights Institute in support of California's proposed Racial Privacy Initiative. Randy told me I couldn't go.

"Well, I'm going."

In July, I scheduled two weeks of seminars in Washington, D.C, at the Leadership Institute and at CATO University. Randy told me I couldn't go.

"Well, I'm going."

I returned to a house with the air conditioning and cable disconnected. "You spend too much money," he said, "so I had to do it."

Randy could make the million-dollar house unlivable, but I didn't have to stay there. I spent the next three days in Glenwood Springs, three hours west of Denver, a Rocky Mountain refuge at the confluence of the Colorado and the Roaring Fork Rivers. I spent those days in the water, submerged in the hot sulfur springs and, via kayak, navigating the rivers nearby.

And thinking about years of being worn down.

Paddle in hand, nestled into the cockpit, I felt the Colorado heave beneath my yellow fiberglass. I let it. It flowed around and beyond, inexorable blue motion—and in control. I let it. At this section of Glenwood Canyon, class III and IV rapids lay ahead, snarling whitecaps and eddies beyond my talent. I paddled just enough to remain in place, well back from the violent churn. I paddled just enough to hold my ground, and the river flowed underneath, a swirl of circumstance and splash, water like years, current like life, a steady tug of roil and obligations and inertia and everything happening to me and around me and at me. Everything pulling me. Years. Life. Husbands.

I did not let it.

I pulled back, strong strokes against the water reminding me of hard, heavy work with hay and steers. I pulled my craft from the flow, my own strength the only engine. With steady, deliberate, methodical strokes I pulled myself to the shore, and out of the water, and onto solid footing.

My destination lay not in the drops and hazards of a whitewater I didn't make, but elsewhere. Somewhere very much else.

Back at the hotel I picked up a glossy flyer from the lobby—Glenwood Springs History. The town was established in 1883, I learned, the year my great-grandfather Emil Linke homesteaded the Granby ranch, a co-pioneer in taming the west and staking one's claim. And it was not called Glenwood Springs at first. That name came two years later, at the urging of a co-founder's wife, who wanted a gentler image, something to elevate the town beyond its reputation for shanties and saloons and brothels.

The town's original name?

Defiance.

———

I packed three suitcases and left behind a magnificent new custom home in an exclusive community of golf and tennis dates with the ladies. I left a shiny sports car and a house of trappings, with Randy trapping the most oppressively of all.

Closing the door, one-way ticket in hand, I surveyed my house for any remaining meaning, any deep attachments not already packed into one of the three suitcases in the taxi's trunk. Anything at all whose keeping would add more value than the psychic weight of carrying it.

I grabbed a cup. "I may need this."

I was traveling alone, but I wasn't alone. Elbows on my knees, waiting at the airport gate, I lowered my head for a silent prayer, "God, guide me, give me courage to—"

My brother Ed called. "This is one of the gutsiest things I have ever seen," he said. "I'm envious of you for taking a new adventure with no fear."

I filled with gratitude and purpose.

That'll do, God.

I left to give myself a chance, in a place where a rugged individualist from Colorado could find a home in spirit, a home as solid underfoot as the Rocky Mountains and as active as their thunderstorms. I left for the most inspiring and positive place I knew, the ticking heart of America. I left for Washington, D.C.

———

"It looks like *Animal House*," I said.

Congressman Bob Beauprez smiled, a broad Colorado dairy farmer's grin. New to the office, but not in a new office, the freshman legislator had just been elected to Colorado's 7th Congressional District, established only two weeks prior as a result of the 2000 U.S. Census, and was now its inaugural representative. Lack of seniority translated to space in the less prestigious Cannon building, fifth floor, its spartan décor turned college-dorm chic, exemplified by receptionist Fez sorting the mail on the entry floor and University of Colorado bumper stickers on the wall behind. I had attended tidier cattle brandings.

"What would you do with the office?" Bob asked, sweeping a hand across the modest interior.

"Can't do much about the view out there," I said. Our windows overlooked a moonscape of rooftop air conditioners. "But in here, for starters, I'd be cleaning up the foyer. The only thing missing is a beer-can pyramid."

My father and his had dealt cattle for over forty years, so our families knew each other for decades. We each understood the difference between the working pasture and the show ring. This office needed to be both.

"Clean up your office and get a professional look. Get up off the floor. It's the United States House of Representatives, not a frat house. That's the start." I scanned the walls. "And some paint. What is this? Scours gray?" The same industrial bluish-white turned every office on the floor into a cold "government happens here" disinvitation.

"Rules, Valery," said Sean Murphy, the Chief of Staff. "The rules of the House, with a capital 'H.' No painting."

"We'll see."

I shared an office with Sean, gatekeeping for the office and maintaining schedules. Like most on Capitol Hill, the Congressman arrived on Monday, worked three days, and left for home on Friday. But I didn't need to leave on Fridays. I was already home.

Easter weekend offered the opportunity for an extended staff lunch, especially with Sean and Bob already out of the office. I called an 11:00 all-hands, and tossed a hundred-dollar bill on the table. "Get a bite, enjoy the weather, and go see the cherry blossoms. You deserve it."

"We can't go without you."

I won the brief test of wills. "Somebody has to answer the phone." Besides, I had work to do. One week prior, I had spotted a well-stocked hardware store only one metro stop away. One day prior, I had stashed three gallons of venetian gold behind my desk. One hour prior, I had informed Roy, from the Architect of the Capitol's office, that our rendezvous would occur as planned.

On the ranch, Walt Gallagher personified the man of action over words. I saw him work alongside Mike McNulty one day, digging posts and building fence. Mike's twin brother Pat had engineered the bunkhouse spittoon pulleys. Strong teen boys my own age, they both outsized Walt, who packed his wiry, Popeye toughness into a frame no more than 120 pounds.

"Kid, move," the old man said.

Walt took Mike's digger and nodded at the youngster to take a breather. Then he demonstrated what work looked like, gouging divots out of unforgiving turf, and spending sweat to prove it.

After a long while, Mike said, "Let me know if you need me to change spots with you."

Walt jammed his tool into the ground. "Boy. Don't you say that." Walt's anger was of the quiet sort, more steam than whistle. "When you're ready to relieve me, just come over and take it."

This office needed a healthy dose of Walt's "Kid, move."

With the staff's footsteps still echoing, I called Roy. He was always more than professionally pleased to hear from me, enough to bend a few rules to aid a damsel in need. A damsel his age. "Now."

He arrived with drop cloths, rollers, tape, and a boyish grin. I locked the office door during working hours for the first time before or since. We hurried pictures and furniture temporarily in the center; tape on the edges; cloth on the floor.

Paint on the walls. Décor replaced.

We unlocked the door. Roy scurried off with the evidence and I dashed to my chair just minutes before the staff returned, time enough for me to commence a furious barrage of typing and paper shuffling.

The staff chatter stopped when they entered the office. The suddenly quiet throng eased through the gold anteroom, sniffing and cautious, to mass at my door. "What's with the—?"

"Hmm?" I looked up, clearly busy with my very important messages to very important people. I gathered an unruly pile of very important papers and squared them with noise and intent.

"The paint? What just happened?"

"Sorry? I don't follow. How was lunch?"

———

Congress is a young person's game. DD still signed notes with a little heart over her name. Kristin asked to wear flip-flops to the office. And both of my little chickadees, the two other women on staff, had boy troubles. They turned to me, the Old Lady on the Hill, for advice.

One chickadee asked if perhaps her new boyfriend was being too controlling. I had some experience in the matter; he was.

"Here's what twenty years of putting yourself second will do," I said. "After that much time on the back burner, nobody knows anymore what you want. You don't know, your boyfriend doesn't know. Randy didn't even know."

The girls perked up at his name; I seldom mentioned my divorce in progress.

"Last year I traveled a lot. Randy didn't like it. Kids were gone, so it was time for me. And yet he tried to smother everything I did to be more independent, especially because I was working for causes—not for him."

They huddled closer for a story. DD poured coffee.

"One night at the kitchen table I'm completely frustrated. I had been waiting twenty years for this, putting kids and the business first.

That was way past long enough, and still he kept fighting me. So I finally ask him, 'What do you want? How do you want me to be?'"

Kristin cut into the banana bread I had brought. It was Monday morning. I brought banana bread every Monday morning.

"In total fury, he slams his fist on the table and shouts, 'I don't know! All I know is that I will *not* wash my own underwear!'"

I let the absurdity and shock resonate.

"What a mama's boy!" said DD.

"You have no idea," I said. "So now it's crystal clear where I stand. The next day I bought him thirty pairs of size thirty-six white jockeys. I packed his drawer full of tighty whities and booked my one-way ticket here. I figured he and I were good for a month."

Lessons with laughter last longer.

In my role as House Mother I sought to instill in the young women a sense of self-respect, the kind that would counter the soft oppression of controlling boyfriends and hormonal lobbyists. This meant that sometimes I emphasized the "Lady" aspect of "Old Lady on the Hill."

"This is Capitol Hill," I said, after another low-cut top threatened the attention span of male co-workers. "The nightclub look has to go. When you walk in this office, you're going to be a professional woman and be taken seriously. No cleavage in here. Go home and zip it up, Honey. Be a lady, but be a smart one."

"Yes, Ma'am."

Congressman Beauprez and the men on staff were not immune to my mission for respect either. Everyone was an appropriate audience for issues of fairness and justice when it came to the boxes.

Our office received numerous surveys, questionnaires, and written interview requests, both for the Congressman and for the staff. Often such requests included the boxes, those bureaucrat-designed, identity-blurring, race-baiting, white-guilty, spoils-chasing, victim-brokering, capricious, sanctimonious, degrading color boxes. Are you black or red or brown or white or yellow? The question is unseemly.

I sent the memo to our entire staff. "Your race is irrelevant to what you think. Just because the box is there does not compel you to check it. This office will not promote the idea of racial inferiority by acknowledging such distinctions in the context of how we believe. Do not check the box."

I hate those boxes. And so when Ward Connerly asked me to be a spokesperson for California's Racial Privacy Initiative in its final push for passage, I talked first to Sean.

"It gets rid of the damn boxes," I said. "Proposition 54 starts with 'The State shall not classify any individual by race' and then gets better. You can't have race preferences if you don't track race."

The Chief of Staff said, "Absolutely. Go. It's only a month until elections out there—and then hurry back. We're not through with you yet."

That step toward a colorblind society became overshadowed by the Gray Davis recall that put Arnold Schwarzenegger into the Governor's chair. With all eyes on the celebrity and crisis, too few heard the message about the value of getting government out of the racial bean-counting business. The Racial Privacy Initiative lost by over two million votes.

Fairness is simple, but it is not easy.

I returned to a full portfolio in Beauprez's "leg shop" (pronounced "ledge"), the work group where staff analyze and advise on legislation under House consideration. My portfolio included Agriculture.

The day before the vote on an appropriations bill, Dr. Dale Jones, our Legislative Director, asked me to review the proposed Hinchey Amendment to that bill, and suggest how to advise the Congressman. I highlighted the relevant text: "None of the funds made available in this Act may be used to prevent Colorado from implementing State laws authorizing the use of medical marijuana."

I told Bob that it was simple. "When you get to its core, you see this is a states' rights issue, not a marijuana issue." He followed my recommendation and voted for the amendment, along with too few of his fellow representatives for its adoption. Nonetheless, two weeks later a gift pack of NORML's "famous recipe" brownies arrived at our door, with instructions to share among the staff.

I made sure the staff stuck to banana bread on company time.

Bob respected the advice of his younger staff, but sometimes those on his team whom life had yet to knock around had not seen enough pitches and come-ons to know when to pull back on the reins. "Everyone in elected office needs someone around to raise the bullshit flag," I told him. "Somebody to tell you and others 'no.' I'll always just lay it on the table."

Even to lobbyists. The AgJOBS bill, an immigration and worker reform bill co-sponsored by Ted Kennedy, loomed on the summer's calendar. In the leg shop, congressional staff are gatekeepers, distilling K Street pitches into actionable summaries for the Representative. Some gates needed aggressive keeping.

"Let me get this straight," I said to the hard-sell lobbyist after his breathless pitch, "I'm a ranch girl, and you're telling me that if this bill passes, that my dad the cattle rancher would have to pay for housing and transportation for these guest workers, and if he doesn't, then my dad, just the little cattle rancher, would get sued."

"Well, yeah."

"In federal court." I had served enough time in federal court for my whole family already.

"It's for worker protection."

"What about farmer protection? I'm not going to tell Congressman Beauprez to vote for this. That's bullsh—that's terrible. We're done."

Lobbyists often got treated with more deference. I didn't do deference.

Later, I told Bob, "Career politicians don't understand this. Your dad the dairy farmer shouldn't get sued for something that workers should provide for themselves. You grew up working the farm; you know the mom and pops out there. Don't vote for this."

He didn't.

Seeing widespread opposition for the bill's amnesty and guest-worker provisions, Speaker Hastert chose to prevent the AgJOBS bill from reaching a floor vote in Congressman Beauprez's 108th Congress. The same bill, in effectively unchanged form, generated considerable debate and compromise in the following three congresses, but it never fixed the burdens placed on family ranches. It remains unpassed.

———

The congressional staff were great kids—full of brilliance and energy— but kids nonetheless. And they belonged on The Hill, with its stress and 24/7 demands. But Congress is also a democracy and a bureaucracy, institutions suited for compromise and procedure. Bob understood right away when I chose to turn in my badge.

"It's a young person's game," I said. "Playing it for a couple years has been plenty. And, well, I'm a little more used to being in control— not just one voice among so many."

I had amplified that voice outside of the congressional office as well, speaking on college campuses to largely unsympathetic audiences: to a black fraternity at the University of North Carolina, whose mass protest of prolonged finger snapping tired their hands more than it diminished my resolve, and on the steps of the University of Michigan's Law School, where boos and hisses from behind angry placards delayed my remarks. I had worked with enough rowdy horses to know that sometimes you need to let them buck and snort to burn off energy. This group, BAMN—By Any Means Necessary, a coalition known for their stridency and enthusiasm—bucked a little longer than most. I smiled and waved from the podium, and spoke once the campus police had hauled them off. After the noise settled, in both Michigan and in North Carolina, I found space for real conversations, one-on-one exchanges with young black men who edged my way once the crowds had dissipated. "Ma'am, could I talk with you regarding what you said about preferences and losing pride?" Those discussions, seeing an individual question the groupthink of racial division, were why I continued to speak, and why I knew that my message needed an audience—an audience unavailable within the strictures and politics of a congressional office.

"I get it," Bob said. "Once you're an entrepreneur, you're independent. It's hard to go work in a bureaucracy. I do get it."

After two terms in the D.C. bureaucracy, Bob Beauprez returned to Colorado to run for governor. He lost.

———

Law student Pat O'Rourke was right when he told me, almost ten years earlier on the Supreme Court plaza, how beautiful this area was, this area near Georgetown and Arlington.

I bought my condominium there, at the Belvedere, with a ninth-floor view of the monuments and the National Mall. It directly overlooks the Iwo Jima Memorial and Arlington National Cemetery.

When Richard Nixon was still president, I visited Washington, D.C., with my parents for the National Cattlemen's Convention. I was a high-school freshman; Ohio guardsmen were yet to kill four students at Kent State. I wore my white patent-leather jacket and matching go-go boots for a wide-eyed tour of our nation's memorials and icons. The green expanses reminded me of home. The reverence for history suggested a broader meaning of "home."

On that trip I saw Arlington National Cemetery for the first time. I stood at John F. Kennedy's gravesite and photographed the Arlington House, just up a gentle slope from the eternal flame. A low stone wall borders the sidewalk that winds south from Robert E. Lee's antebellum home, and on the walk's eastern curve, up the manicured hill from JFK's gravesite, is a perch. Discovering this resting place years later, after I worked in the city, convinced me to live nearby. From this vantage, with the flame below, the view extends across the Potomac to a verdant canopy of oak and hickory, above which rises the Washington Monument, resolution cut from American stone. The capitol building juts through the haze beyond, its dome a reminder of the cupola within, where our country's heritage is memorialized in frieze and fresco. Atop it, visible only as a suggestion from this distance, stands the Statue of Freedom. Lady Freedom faces east, towards the rising sun and the Supreme Court just across the street.

But nearby is sanctity. As much as the vista expresses freedom, the closeness, Arlington itself, represents sacrifice. Here lie over 400,000, our freedom purchased with their lives. I thank them.

This low wall, this view, this feeling of reverence and gratitude, is, next to the ranch, my favorite place on earth. Here is my solemn sanctuary, where I come to write and to think and to pray.

And I will until I die.

"Fairy Tale, We're Not"

CHAPTER FOURTEEN

This Is America

"Look 'em in the eye—and listen."

I grew up with two homes, the bubble of Kremmling and the toil of Granby, and I needed both.

And as much as I loved the focus of Washington, D.C., I missed the rustic connections of the family homestead. It was time to trade shoveling political manure on the east coast for shoveling actual manure in the Rocky Mountains again. Without giving up my home at the Belvedere, but only renting it out until the time came to return, I decided to come back to Colorado.

A true friend helps you move. I rang up Squid, my part-time college roommate and intermittent pen pal. I never, ever called her Susan, not since her basketball skills appeared to me to stem from having too many arms. Everyone else dropped the nickname for her after college; I never did.

"Squid. It's Orr." We needed few words to communicate, ever since our days as the battery on our UNC softball team. She pitched and I caught, which meant that during our games I flashed the signals—

most often a one-finger salute, since we didn't really know any proper hand gestures, but we found that one sufficed for most circumstances anyway. "Road trip? I'm bringing some things from my condo back to Colorado, and wanted to do a little treasure hunting along the way."

"I could use a lamp. I'm in."

At the Green Dragon Pub, in Bilbo Baggins Global Restaurant, in Old Town Alexandria, Squid and I ordered another. Moving out was thirsty work.

"So now we have a full truck. Now what?" Squid said. Our big truck squatted on the narrow cobblestones, bulging out of its confines like a parent squeezed into a child's school desk. After loading it with over-flow from my condo, we topped it off with irresistible finds from Deco-rium, our favorite furniture, curio, and design store, owned by Jeff, and run by Cory and David, our favorite fussy, mincing, and talented designers.

"Full? Decorium isn't empty yet, and you still have room on your lap."

Cory had sent us here, a short walk from their store, for after-shopping crowd watching and the best cheese hors d'oeuvres in town. He failed to mention the potential for entreaties from roving peacocks.

Maverick was a pretty boy, driving a pretty Porsche, parked close enough so that, from our window seats, we could not miss his puff and strut. On the way in, and once inside, he demonstrated that some people do, in fact, saunter. It is not an effective means of locomotion or attraction.

"Ladies." He pitched his voice at us, a fake half-octave low. "I'm Jim. My friends call me Maverick."

"Squid, did I ever tell you how my brother Ed describes a maverick on the ranch?" This conversation wouldn't take long. I was fine leaving Maverick in momentary limbo.

"Do tell, Orr."

"Turns out it's a calf whose mama died, and then its daddy, once it saw the young'un, up and took off with another cow. Ain't nobody loves a maverick. Nobody."

Pretty Boy squinted at us, then wandered off, his puzzled expression reminiscent of a freshly branded calf's. To his back, Squid and I muttered, "No. Just no."

Laughter is contagious.

"Might we join you?" A trio from a nearby table watched with us as Jim worked his way back through the crowd, his stops elsewhere as brief as at our table. "We thought perhaps without Maverick for company you might get lonely."

Aussie couple Shane and Bendee had just moved to D.C. for his job as Chief of Staff for the ABCA Armies, a military coalition to standardize operations between American, British, Canadian, and Australian forces. Wife Bendee was an artist and former hog farmer. Brit Heather had been in the states for two years on behalf of the ABCA. All three of them were testing the pub's considerable on-tap selection.

A convivial hour became an evening of sudden friends, with me dispensing hometown advice on proper neighborhoods, military and political connections, and art galleries for the Aussies, and Squid and I both offering frontier counsel for Heather, whose marital woes had come forth as the pint glasses kept getting refilled.

"But he doesn't do anything. He won't work," Heather said, suggesting an obstacle of bewildering immensity.

Squid looked Heather square in the eyes. "Tell him to go get a job."

Heather tried to elaborate. "It's not that easy—"

Squid and I both laughed, a clear and exuberant release. "Maybe not," I said. "But it really is simple. Tell him exactly that, and don't let anything else complicate the issue." Like I did for twenty-five years.

Some things are simple. Most things are simple.

As we closed the bar that night, I held my empty glass up for

Squid's inspection, and pointed at the tavern's logo. "This. Right here," I said. "That's our view of the world, and overdue."

It said, "Fairy Tale, We're Not."

—————

After three hundred miles and a reverent tour of Jefferson's Monticello estate, we ended our first day on the road at The Texas Steakhouse and Saloon, in Martinsville, Virginia, where Rosie Red served us good steaks. We told her so.

Her instant smile illuminated a complexion that had just started to age well, ruddy and enduring. Tiny, she moved more with grace and efficiency than exuberance. She's done this many, many times before, and steadily. Reliably. Comfortably. Invisibly.

When she brought our second round and cleared the plates, she said, "You two are having quite the good time. Giggling like school-girls all night."

"We are spreading joy across the state it seems," I said. "We are just joyful people."

"I could use a dose of that."

Squid glanced down next to her. "You can sit here with us. There's always room."

When Rosie Red's shift ended we had a new friend. A new friend with two small children, pictures of whom she unfolded on our table, along with her story. "Every summer. Tennessee with his family. He's the one who cooked your steaks."

We listened. So many people don't.

"It's not like I don't love my in-laws, but it's every summer. And maybe it's my heritage—Crow Nation—but I feel attached to this place. And I want our kids to feel that too, here in Virginia."

I knew that attachment, a visceral psychic draw, a ceaseless reminder of beginnings and endings.

Manager Bruce stopped by. "And how is everything tonight?" His smile pointed at us but his eyes accused Rosie Red.

Squid's turn. "Rosie here is a fantastic waitress, making our evening better with her company. And her husband does a perfect medium-rare."

My turn. "You need more people like her. She's very conscientious. In my considered opinion as a connoisseur of fine wait staff, I recommend that she be given a raise."

"I'll see what I can do," he said, lighting up as he walked away, as if he had taken a little of our joy with him, and diminished our supply not at all.

"Just joyful people," said Squid.

I turned to Rosie Red. "Here's your dose of cowgirl advice."

She leaned closer.

I said, "If you don't want to go, don't go."

Rosie paused for a moment, then sat up a little straighter.

Squid and I were of a mind. She said, "It's not complicated. Don't go."

Whether Rosie had ever considered the idea before, she was considering it now. I said, "You stay. The kids stay. He goes. Simple."

She half chuckled, a small gasp of possibility. "I might just."

Trust yourself. Most things are simple.

The next morning, Tim Martin opened his family-owned wholesale furniture warehouse early for us, knowing that today's Nashville destination meant a full day on the road. Years of outfitting my condo, as well as sending custom pieces back to Colorado, granted me special privilege when I passed through Martinsville, which I made a habit of doing. I told Squid that the city was named for Tim's ancestor Joseph Martin, Revolutionary war hero and close friend of Patrick Henry. "'Bout five 'greats' tween me and him," Tim said. "That means I got plenty of cousins to pick from."

He walked us through the showroom, a private tour of eclecticism and quality. "Let's see what we can squeeze in your truck, Darlin'."

Tim's lamp for Squid and framed image of our founders signing the Declaration of Independence for me—complete with quill pen—put our truck beyond current capacity.

His aw-shucks drawl downplayed the pretension of Martinsville's abundance of millionaires, his family included. "It's just old country. Old money don't matter. Not 'round here. 'Round here we're all the same, just rednecks waiting for the next NASCAR race." Old-moneyed rednecks whose town history included "plug tobacco capital of the world" among its distinctions and, in later years, "sweatshirt capital of the world," but yet which still boasted some of the finest furniture on the east cost.

After helping rearrange our cargo to squeeze in our finds, Tim gave us explicit directions to cross the Blue Ridge Mountains the long way around. "You can't take the shortcut. It's 'em hill boys. They're like to take a shine to ya."

An hour out of Martinsville, Tim rang us up.

"This is a beautiful drive," I told him. "We just got a spectacular picture of Lovers' Leap."

"Oh, Lordy, darlins. That means you missed 220 and went over the hills. You're in Rocky Knob now," he said. "You prolly shouldn't ought to be getting out your truck for the next hour."

Tim's back-country advice kept us inside our vehicle as we passed through the last of the one-corner towns on the Jeb Stuart Highway. Under an antique "Antique" sign, a local denizen sprawled across his recliner, atop his ramshackle porch, surrounded by rubble. Likely he meant for the Appalachian detritus all around him—the attic leftovers, discarded plumbing, and rusty structures held up by more rust—to be his establishment's wares. They might instead have been an annex to the local landfill.

I was behind the wheel. "Squid, what's the difference between antique and junk?"

"If you can offer it up without people laughing that it's for sale, it's antique. So his sign is wrong."

"Get your camera out. I'm slowing down for a picture. And I think he's smiling at us, but I can't see his teeth from here."

"Orr, you can't see his teeth from anywhere."

We laughed all the way to Tennessee.

———

Once we left Nashville, we copied Sparky's homing inclinations and ran for the barn, but even a single-minded horse needs to stop for a drink if the ride is long enough. We put our boots back on the ground in Hays, Kansas, at the Whiskey Creek Grill.

Another day's travel unwound with steaks, beer, and laughter, especially with home only a day away. Tonight's server lingered a little long as she set our foamy pints in place. A subtle head shake and a wistful smile suggested that she would rather be tipping them up instead of setting them down.

"You look like you should join us," offered Squid.

"I wish." She looked early twenties. Attractive. Busy. "Not while I'm under this boss's thumb." She bustled off as if tethered to the kitchen.

On her next circuit, I said, "Got troubles? Sit down and we'll buy you a beer." By now we had abandoned all inhibitions; we assumed that everyone we met was already a close friend asking our advice.

She leaned over, one arm on the table, both to rest and to bring us into her confidence. "Don't take it personal, but I'm just fed up with this job."

Squid's counsel was right between the eyes. "Well, go get a new job."

"Simple," I chimed in.

"It's not that easy."

I chuckled. The same sentiment from everyone. "Honey, I did not say it was easy. I said it was simple."

She glanced around, aware of her delay, scanning for workplace censure. Now her face showed intrigue. All across the country people were drawn to us, eager to hear someone sidestep their negativity as naturally as we ignored the emotional moats they had dug around themselves.

"Here's the difference," I said. "Simple means clear, you know what has to be done. Maybe doing it's not easy, maybe getting there is hard. But they're not the same."

My fight for equality was simple: fair is fair. But it was not easy.

Squid said, "We have to do things every day that aren't easy. That's the hard work we all do, all the time. But doing that hard work for the right reason—like getting the job you really want—that, my dear, is simple."

We were pied pipers, our tune one that granted permission to people who shouldn't have to ask for it, leaving in our wake a handful of new friends willing to consider that obvious problems might call for the most obvious answers.

She was fully curious and amused. "Where in the world did you two come from?"

"America."

———

Just west of our Granby ranch house, the sinuous ridgeline dips into a natural saddle, a formation whose shape includes a seat, stirrups, and, at its highest ridge, a horn. On that pinnacle stands one tree, a weathered and defiant lodgepole pine, reliably thriving since well before my childhood, and accessible only on horseback or a long morning's pilgrimage on foot.

I came home to this solitary ground, a parallel sanctuary to my Arlington post. A visit to the saddle means enduring chill winds in exchange for expansive vistas: the Continental Divide cresting in three directions, hazy miles north, east, and south. I never begrudge the cost.

My mother has always referred to this place as "that windswept ridge where nature favors no man." I see it as my perch above America, a silent lookout on centuries of pioneering, on exercising human will to purpose, as a spiritual haven of rock and hope.

Lodgepole pine can live up to 400 years. I suspect this arboreal sentry of coming into its middle age, its vigil long enough to witness the Ute tribe convening their summer camps; my great-grandfather clearing the heath of rocks and sagebrush with a horse and his bare hands; my grandfather irrigating the Timothy hay with nothing more than a shovel and his will; my mother trotting on her horse to the one-room schoolhouse; and me working the hayfield, moving cattle, and racing my horse across the lush meadow beneath, laying in the cat's-tail grass and clover, watching the clouds drift and billow overhead, and dreaming big dreams.

One-room schoolhouse, early 1900s

CHAPTER FIFTEEN

Lagniappe

"Lagniappe: an extra bonus or unexpected gift given with a purchase."

ORIGIN: LOUISIANA FRENCH

You know those "where are they now?" snippets you sometimes see at the end of true-life movies? I love those. I hope you do too.

Jack and Alta Orr summered for years at the family ranch in Granby and spent their winters in Westminster. Alta is feistier than ever and describes herself, with a sly grin, as an "intolerably mean granny." She's lying; we can tolerate her. Jack Orr resides at the Grace Pointe Continuing Care Senior Campus, in Greeley, Colorado. He watches more TV than he used to.

Kendra Pech resides in Colorado.

Ted Pech is a chef living in San Francisco with his wife, Courtney.

William Perry Pendley remains president of Mountain States Legal Foundation, which returned to the Supreme Court for its October,

2013 term on behalf of a Wyoming man whose property was seized by the federal government. They won. Perry has just published his fourth book, *Sagebrush Rebel: Reagan's Battle With Environmental Extremists and Why It Matters Today* (Regnery, 2013). He lives in Evergreen, Colorado with his wife, Lis. They have two children. He shaved his mustache.

Todd Welch is counsel for the Pikes Peak Regional Building Department. He describes his time with Mountain States Legal Foundation as a gift, as the whole reason he went to law school, as something good for America. He tears up when he says it, and he knows it's corny. That's why I'm so fond of Todd. He displays his "Equal Justice Under Law" marble block in his living room.

Pat O'Rourke serves as Vice President, University Counsel and Secretary of the Board of Regents of the University of Colorado. He got an A on the opinion he wrote on Adarand v. Peña for his Georgetown law school seminar.

Ed Jones is a former county commissioner, state senator and longtime Republican Party activist. A stint in the Army lifted him out of racist, small-town Mississippi and took him to Colorado, where he stayed after leaving the military in the early 1960s. Ed and his wife, B.J., make their home in Colorado Springs. He hosts a weekly radio show. As a state senator, he sponsored legislation to eliminate racial preferences in state government. It lost by one vote.

Pat McNulty is an author and award-winning radio and television broadcaster living in Centennial, Colorado, with his wife, Carol. They have three children. His book, *Great Music Radio.com*, takes much of its inspiration from my family's homesteaded ranch in Granby. He frequently contributes to *Playboy's Party Jokes*, drawing on boys-only chatter exchanged as a teen in the ranch's bunkhouse.

Mike McNulty is an insurance auditor who lives in Denver, but spends most of his time flying across the country, making state governments and insurance companies play nice together. He and his twin brother credit summers bucking bales at the Orr ranch for solidifying their work ethic and helping lead them to successful careers—careers that don't call for being on their feet twelve hours a day.

Tim McWilliams lives in Roggen, Colorado and is a Captain for Frontier Airlines. He retired from the Air Force Reserve after twenty-two years of service, including tours in Iraq and Afghanistan. He has one daughter. Tim still reads aviator magazines.

Gary McMahan is featured in the upcoming documentary, *Everything in this Song is True*. He lives with his wife, Candace, and a couple of good dogs at the mouth of a canyon in Northern Colorado. Gary tours nationally, singing, telling stories, and yodeling for his supper. He was the Best Man at Clair's wedding. Under the influence of Jack Daniels on the rocks, and when no children are in the audience, he swears with flabbergasting creativity.

Walt Gallagher stopped returning from skid row in 1977.

Nona Crane lives in Granby, Colorado, with her husband, Jeff. They have one child. She owns Altitude Trophy & Awards and Coulter House Engraving, both meant to create and preserve everlasting memories. She still calls me her little buddy. I still call her my bestest buddy.

Mona Wahlert lives in Fort Morgan, Colorado with her husband, Dave. They have one child. Raised on a ranch in Kremmling, she swore when she left that she would never look at another cow. Instead, she has worked for almost three decades at Superior Livestock, the nation's largest auction house, marketing over one million head of cattle each year. Neither she nor I can ever tolerate eating canned chili again.

Aunt Jean Hinman lives in Fort Morgan, Colorado, where she works part-time at Superior Livestock and still laughs about our Goldwater hijinks.

Mitch and Gina are still helluva hands on the ranch.

Gary Simpson lives in Colorado Springs with his wife, Sylvia. He has two children. After six years in the Air Force, he now works in the Department of Defense as a contracting officer, where he allocates contracts to firms based on their status as small, disadvantaged businesses. He is still funny and charming and shy and strong and fast. I will always love him for the man he is and for the barriers we broke in 1971. He carries a 230 average.

Rachel Legg is a retired schoolteacher living in Colorado Springs with her husband, Keith. They have three children from international adoptions. She never lost her love of music, performing, and dance that she developed in her years with Sing Out Colorado Springs.

Joe Nance lives in Virginia with his wife and two children. He runs spy satellites. I can't say more.

The One-Room Schoolhouse built by Emil Linke has been restored to its early 20th-century configuration and moved to be a permanent display in the Grand County Museum. A boys-only bunkhouse when I was growing up, the structure had originally been the education hub for local ranch kids, my mother included. After its bunkhouse demotion, the log structure later found historian sponsors with long civic memories. They repaired all of the bullet holes.

Jeff Buerger sells Colorado ranches as a partner at Hall & Hall, using industry experience gained from working alongside Jack Orr for a decade. During past summers he fought bulls, flew combat aircraft, and raced sport bikes. He founded Aerial Imaging Productions, now in its seventh year of operations. Jeff is still the man I want next to me in a dust-up.

Ray Hart is a real estate appraiser living in Golden, Colorado. I love him like a brother.

Ed Orr lives in Greeley, Colorado with his wife, Susie. They have one child. The boy I beat up is now the man who is a best friend. I love him like a brother.

Fred Orr lives in Denver, Colorado with his wife, Coleen. They have three children. He still thinks twice about tasting whipped cream. I love him like a brother.

Clair Orr lives in Kersey, Colorado with his wife, Deb. They have three children and six grandchildren. He lives life like a Hardy Boys adventure. I love him like a brother.

Ray Shoop sees more clearly with one eye than most see with two, and is the most Godly, selfless man I know. He manages Ed Orr's ranch, there carrying on the Orr tradition of giving young men opportunities the city life cannot.

Ward Connerly continues, on behalf of the American Civil Rights Institute, to fight to remove racial preferences and the individual indignities they foster. He lives in Sacramento, California.

Bob Beauprez and his wife, Claudia, have four children. He splits time between his home in Lafayette, Colorado, and his buffalo ranch in Walden, Colorado. Bob remains politically active and is the editor-in-chief of *A Line of Sight*, an online policy resource.

Mike Cunningham stockpiles small arms and grows marijuana at an undisclosed commune in southern Oregon. His young, common-law wife smokes meth and has few teeth.

Nicole Retland lives in Washington D.C. and works at Howard University, where she is pursuing her Ph.D. in microbiology. Her grandmother just graduated from college. Nicole is still a shining star, as charming, brilliant, and delightful as the day she testified on the Colorado Senate floor in seventh grade. When I asked her what has led to her success as an adult, she ticked off four items: God, family, intelligence, and drive. I said to her, "You never mentioned affirmative action."

Squid is called Susan Beryl Rector by others, *apparently*. She recently returned to her small hometown of Deer Trail, Colorado, "Home of the World's First Rodeo." From that base camp she makes a living with a paintbrush in hand, and continues her road-trip quest to drive all of the 120 Most Scenic Drives in America.

Valery Orr drinks beer from her "Fairy Tale, We're Not" pint glass, which she keeps in the freezer. She is joyful.

My three brothers and I now own **The Homestead Ranch** in Granby.

The Bar O Brand remains a family treasure, an ongoing reminder to blaze one's message clear and accept no barriers.

Made in the USA
San Bernardino, CA
31 August 2014